Brother, Whatever You Do, Please Don't Marry This Woman!

A Lesson from Marrying the Wrong Woman

Author – Eld Joel Latimore Jr.

Brother, Whatever You Do, Please Don't Marry This Woman!

A Lesson from Marrying the Wrong Woman

Published by Latimore Publishing

ISBN (Paperback): 979-8-218-83951-2

Printed in the United States of America

Scripture Notice: Unless otherwise noted, all Scripture quotations are from the King James Version (KJV) of the Bible, which is in the public domain.

Disclaimer: This book reflects the author's personal testimony, opinions, and pastoral counsel. It is not intended as a substitute for professional legal, medical, or psychological advice.

Portions of this material were previously published in **Not This Woman: Delilah's Spirit, the Strange Woman, and the Cost of Compromise**. This work expands upon and revises those earlier writings.

Requests for permission, ministry inquiries, or bulk orders:

Email: elderjoellatimore@yahoo.com

Cover design by ChatGPT

Interior layout by the author

10 9 8 7 6 5 4 3 2 1

Author's Note

This book was written with a burden—not of bitterness, but of responsibility. Too many men, both in the Church and in the military, have fallen prey to the same unseen enemy: the spirit that hides behind *charm, beauty, and attention.* The Bible calls her the strange woman—and her influence is still destroying *callings, marriages, reputations, careers,* and *futures today.*

The image on the cover is not intended to offend, stereotype, or misrepresent any race or culture. It is **a symbol**—a visual representation of spiritual deception. The contrast of light and darkness reflects the inward struggle between truth and temptation, purity and compromise. It portrays the reality that sin often presents itself as beautiful, yet beneath its appearance lies bondage and destruction. The message is spiritual, not racial; it exposes a condition of the heart, not the color of the skin.

Brother, Whatever You Do, Please Don't Marry This Woman is not about one individual; it is about a spirit. It's about the seductive nature of sin that appears desirable but is deadly to a man's purpose. Every chapter is written to expose how this spirit operates, how it gains access, and how it cripples the spiritual and moral authority of men who are anointed or respected—but unguarded.

I write these words as a man who once thought he was strong enough to handle what God had already warned me to flee. I was a fool to believe that I could date or marry someone of that caliber and come out unharmed. Pride and self-confidence blinded me to wisdom.

I thought I could fix what was broken, discern what was hidden, and survive what others did not. But sin does not negotiate—it destroys. The spirit behind such a woman is not impressed by your uniform, your title, or your ministry. It only seeks to dismantle your character, silence your voice, and drain your strength.

Please, my brothers—whether you stand behind a pulpit or serve in uniform—don't make the same mistake I made by marrying or entertaining a woman who embodies this spirit. What begins as fascination ends as bondage, and the cost is always greater than you expect to pay.

This is also a message to both the Church and the military community. For too long, we have avoided the kind of conversations that could have saved countless men from silent destruction. We have celebrated authority while neglecting accountability.

We have mistaken emotional attraction for divine assignment. The result has been a trail of broken families, compromised missions, and men who lost their purpose in the very environments where they were meant to lead.

Men, I write to you not as one who has always been strong, but as one who learned through scars. The Holy Ghost is still able to deliver, restore, and realign your destiny.

The lessons in these pages are not theories—they are the fruit of experience and divine correction. My prayer is that what cost me years of pain will spare you the same.

To the Church and the military community, I pray this book rekindles the courage to confront spiritual deception with holiness, truth, and integrity.

When we expose darkness, we give light a chance to heal. If you read these words with humility and reflection, you will see that this is not just a warning—it's a call to return to purity, discipline, wisdom, and spiritual vigilance.

Eld Joel Latimore Jr.

2025

Dedication

This book is dedicated to every man who has ever been deceived by what looked like love but was really a trap.

To every brother—preacher, soldier, husband, or leader—who discovered too late that the enemy doesn't always come with a weapon, but sometimes with a smile.

To the men who are rebuilding after betrayal, and to those who are still trying to understand how they got here—this book is for you.

To the Church and the military community who have carried the weight of silent struggles, may these pages break that silence and bring healing through truth.

And to the women who read this book with humility and reflection, may you see the power of redemption and the beauty of becoming who God designed you to be.

Above all, this book is dedicated to the Lord Jesus Christ, who delivered me from deception, restored my mind, and taught me that true strength begins with surrender.

Eld Joel Latimore Jr.

2025

Preface

This book was not written from theory, but from experience, correction, and revelation. I have seen firsthand how the same destructive spirit operates in both the Church and the military—seducing good men, silencing strong leaders, and destroying families. What began as my personal lesson has become a divine assignment: to warn, to teach, and to call men back to discipline and discernment.

We live in a time when charm overshadows character and pleasure is mistaken for purpose. The strange woman of Proverbs is not an ancient story—her spirit still moves today, hunting unguarded men who carry promise and calling. She disguises herself as affection, attention, and emotional support, but her true intent is to drain strength and corrupt destiny.

As both a soldier and a preacher, I have watched men fall in different uniforms—some wearing medals, others wearing collars. The enemy doesn't care about your title; he only cares about your weakness. That is why spiritual vigilance is no longer optional—it's survival.

This book is not written to condemn but to awaken. It is a call for men to wake up, for the Church to confront deception, and for women to rediscover the beauty of godly influence and redemption. The lessons you will read were born from failure, refined by grace, and written to protect others from the same pit.

My prayer is that these pages strengthen you to walk in purity, discipline, and wisdom—because what you don't confront will eventually consume you.

Eld Joel Latimore Jr.

2025

Table of Contents

- Author's Note

- Dedication

- Preface

Introduction: The Spirit Behind the Smile

You may think she's just confident. You may think she's just bold. You may even think she's your answer from God.

But what if she's a distraction? What if she's a setup? What if she's a hinderance to your ministry?

There is a woman described in the Book of Proverbs—one whose intentions are not pure, and whose allegiance is not to God. Scripture calls her the strange woman **(Proverbs 2:16–19; 5:3–6; 7:5–27).**

She flatters with her words, entices with her eyes, and leads men—not just into sin—but into spiritual ruin.

"For by means of a whorish woman a man is brought to a piece of bread: and the adulteress will hunt for the precious life."

— **Proverbs 6:26**

This book is about her.

Not a woman with a specific name, but a woman with a specific spirit. The one whose mission aligns with Satan's: *to steal, to kill, and to destroy* **(John 10:10).**

She doesn't come to love—she comes to weaken. She doesn't come to build—she comes to tear down.

She is not just in the streets; she is often seated in churches, dressed in modesty, camouflaged in titles, but carrying poison in her lips and rebellion in her heart.

This is a serious matter, especially for men in the church and those serving in the military—two environments where strength, silence, and service often overshadow vulnerability and spiritual discernment.

And yet, this subject is rarely addressed from the pulpit. Many preachers refuse to touch it. They avoid confronting what could save a generation of men from destruction. But I cannot remain silent.

I will talk about it.

I will warn and expose the spirit that lures men—young and old—into entanglements that cost them their purpose, their purity, and their peace.

I will reveal the traps, the setups, and the seductions that are not just natural—they are spiritual. Because the Bible has much to say about it.

Samson's dilemma with Delilah wasn't just a moral failure—it was a prophetic picture of what many men called to ministry will one day face if they are not careful.

I know this firsthand. In my previous book **Faith and Fire: Walking with the Holy Ghost**, I shared the crippling emotional and spiritual ordeal I experienced with two women—Kelly and Jo—as I tried to walk in the call of God on my life.

I was a soldier in the U.S. Army. A man trying to serve both my country and my God. But I was *emotionally vulnerable, spiritually unprepared,* and *relationally entangled* with a woman sent to hinder my ministry.

Kelly wasn't just a mistake—she was a manifestation of the warning found in Proverbs.

She infiltrated my life, influenced my finances, corrupted my home, and stood as a direct obstacle to the call of God on my life. I married her when I should have walked away.

And the Lord warned me in a vision: *"She is not mine. She is a whore."* His words, not mine. And still, I didn't listen.

The result? *Years of delay. Emotional torment. Spiritual confusion. And courtroom injustice.*

But even in that storm, God spoke deliverance. He said, *"If you marry her, she will hinder your ministry."*

I replied, But Lord, after she do this will You kill her? He said, *"No, but I will deliver you."* And He did.

This book is also about the many Samsons— mighty men with divine callings, set apart from birth, filled with potential and anointing—who have been *delayed, derailed, or even destroyed* because they trusted the wrong woman with their secrets… and laid their heads in the wrong lap.

Samson wasn't weak. He was chosen. He was called. But he was also *vulnerable—emotionally exhausted and spiritually distracted.*

And like many men today, he didn't lose his strength in battle. He lost it in the arms of someone who was secretly aligned with his enemy.

Delilah was not just a woman—she was a weapon. So was Jezebel. And their spirits are still working today, seducing prophets, neutralizing warriors, and silencing voices that were called to set nations free.

This spirit doesn't just seduce—it studies. It doesn't just flirt—it infiltrates.

It learns your patterns, studies your wounds, and disguises itself as everything you've prayed for—only to snatch the very thing God gave you.

If you are not spiritually awake, this spirit will slip into your bed, your leadership team, your church, your home—and ultimately, your destiny.

There is a reason the Bible repeatedly warns against the strange woman. She is not just a physical danger—she is a spiritual assassin. Her beauty blinds, her words flatter, and her path leads to death.

"A foolish woman is clamorous: she is simple, and knoweth nothing. For she sitteth at the door of her house… To call passengers who go right on their ways: Whoso is simple, let him turn in hither… But he knoweth not that the dead are there; and that her guests are in the depths of hell."

— **Proverbs 9:13–18**

The Bible doesn't say this young man was evil—only that he was *simple*. He lacked discernment. He was unguarded. He was likely looking for affection or excitement… and it cost him his life.

This is the warning for every man reading this book: One moment of blindness can cost you your calling.

One night in the wrong bed can set your destiny back decades. You don't have to be wicked to be destroyed—you just have to be unwise.

How many gifted men have died with unfulfilled potential because they trusted what they could see instead of what they should have discerned?

This book is not written to condemn you—it's written to wake you up. Because not every *"good woman"* is a God woman. And not every invitation is a blessing.

Let me be clear: This book is not a license to bash women.

It is a trumpet blast to expose the spirit that hides behind beauty, behind confidence, behind titles and tears—and works undercover to dismantle the callings of great men and infiltrate the gates of the church.

It is a warning to the wandering. A mirror to the blind. A weapon in the hands of the wounded.

Because once you discern the spirit behind the smile, you will never fall for the same lie again.

Chapter 1: Delilah Was Never in Love

"For by means of a whorish woman a man is brought to a piece of bread: and the adulteress will hunt for the precious life."

— Proverbs 6:26 (KJV)

This chapter is not written to shame anyone, but to awaken every man of God who thinks he can handle what only the Holy Ghost can conquer.

Delilah was never in love—she was on assignment. Her goal was not affection; it was **assassination**. Her words were soft, but her mission was spiritual. Many men have fallen because they confused emotional attention with divine approval.

Every man who carries purpose will, **at some point, face a Delilah**. She may not wear the same face, but the spirit is the same—*strategic, patient, and destructive.* It studies your weaknesses, waits for your weariness, and strikes when you're least guarded. The goal is always the same: to cut your hair, blind your eyes, silence your strength, and steal your money.

I know this battle personally. I was one of those men who believed my anointing was strong enough to keep me safe. I thought discernment was automatic simply because I was called to preach, pray, and serve. But sin doesn't care about your calling; the enemy only needs a moment of disobedience to dismantle a divine mission.

This book was written as both a warning and a witness—to show that no man is beyond temptation, and no calling is safe without vigilance.

Delilah represents more than a woman; she represents a system—*designed to drain, distract, and destroy.* When a man ignores wisdom, he becomes his own worst enemy.

If you read these pages with humility, you will see not just the danger of Delilah, but the mercy of God. Because even when we fail, grace still rebuilds. The goal is not to shame men, but to sharpen them—to help them see what's coming before it's too late.

There is perhaps no story in Scripture more tragic and revealing about the power of seduction than the fall of Samson at the hands of Delilah.

His story, as recorded in **Judges 13–16,** is not just a tale of betrayal—it is a spiritual blueprint for understanding the war that rages over the destiny of men.

Samson was not an ordinary man. He was chosen from the womb, consecrated as a Nazarite, and filled with divine strength. He was born with a *divine mission*—to begin the deliverance of Israel from the hand of the Philistines **(Judges 13:5).**

He was set apart to wage war not just in the physical, but as a vessel of God's power and judgment against Israel's oppressors. Yet despite such a holy calling, Samson repeatedly compromised his mission by pursuing relationships with *ungodly women.*

From the woman in Timnah to the harlot in Gaza, and finally Delilah, his pattern revealed a fatal flaw—a heart drawn to what God warned against.

The trajectory of Samson's life is a cautionary tale: each woman he pursued moved him further from his divine assignment and deeper into enemy territory.

What began as small compromises escalated into covenant-breaking disobedience. Samson was raised to be a judge and deliverer, but he allowed desire to cloud discernment.

"There is a way that seemeth right unto a man, but the end thereof are the ways of death."

— Proverbs 14:12

Samson followed what felt right, not what was righteous—and it cost him everything. Despite his physical power, he had a spiritual weakness: he lacked discernment when it came to women.

His life became a drama of contrasts—***strength*** *and weakness,* ***calling*** *and compromise,* ***anointing*** *and vulnerability.*

He did not lose to an army; he lost in a bedroom. His downfall did not come through battle—it came through intimacy with a woman whose loyalty was never to him, but to his enemies.

Delilah was not in love. **She was on assignment.**

Wisdom Key: *A woman sent by Satan will always ask for the part of you that God told you to protect.*

The book of Proverbs repeatedly warns against this kind of woman:

"With her much fair speech she caused him to yield, with the flattering of her lips she forced him. He goeth after her straightway... till a dart strike through his liver."

— Proverbs 7:21–23

Delilah was not merely seductive—she was strategic. She studied him. She wore him down. She didn't use force—she used **patience.** The betrayal came not through violence but through **persistence**.

Delilah's strength was in her persistence, which mirrored Samson's weakness in resisting her.

And just like the strange woman in Proverbs, Delilah's bed was not a place of love—it was a **grave.**

"Her house is the way to hell, going down to the chambers of death."

— Proverbs 7:27

Samson trusted the wrong woman with the right secret. His strength was not just in his hair—it was in his obedience to the vow.

"Give not that which is holy unto the dogs, neither cast ye your pearls before swine, lest they trample them under their feet, and turn again and rend you."

— Matthew 7:6

Samson cast his pearls—his sacred anointing, his God-ordained strength—before someone who was never worthy of the revelation. This verse is not just about speech—it's about stewardship.

What God gives us to guard; we must not give away cheaply. And once Delilah discovered that secret, she sold him out for silver.

It has been rightly said that the enemy will always attack where you are most gifted if you are not grounded where you are most vulnerable.

Samson's gift was strength. His weakness was *loneliness, desire,* and *emotional fatigue.* That is the recipe for spiritual assassination.

The soul is the battleground. If Satan can gain influence there, he can control even the most spiritual man. Samson had the Spirit upon him—but lacked discipline within. He was powerful on the outside but weakened on the inside.

This is where the Jezebel and Delilah spirits operate—in the realm of emotional and spiritual fatigue. These spirits don't just seduce—*they study, wear down, and wait until you're too tired to resist.*

"He told her all his heart…"

— **Judges 16:17**

And that's where the war was lost. Not in battle—but in conversation. In the wrong bed. With the wrong woman.

Wisdom Key: *What you give your heart to; you give your strength to.*

Many men in the Church and even in the military—strong, trained, disciplined—have found themselves disarmed by Delilah-like spirits that didn't look like threats. They looked like comfort. They looked like connection. But they were setups.

Delilah never prayed with Samson. She never sacrificed for him. She only pursued him when she was offered a reward. We must ask ourselves: Why are we laying our heads in laps that have no intention of helping us fulfill our mission and our calling?

True spiritual power is not measured by emotion or performance, but by discernment and obedience. A man without the Holy Ghost is a man without eyes.

Samson had strength, but no spiritual vision. That's how he ended up blind in both the spirit and the natural.

"But the Philistines took him, and put out his eyes…"

— Judges 16:21

Delilah did not take his strength—she simply revealed where it lived. It was Samson who handed it over.

Wisdom Key: *If the enemy cannot beat you with force, he will befriend you through seduction.*

Let every man called by God take heed. Delilah is still working. Jezebel is still plotting. And the strange woman still hunts for the precious life.

The story of Samson is more than a historical account—it is an **allegory.** It reveals how a man, filled with potential and consecrated for divine purpose, can forfeit everything when seduction enters where discipline is absent.

Delilah is not just a woman—she is a type. A shadow of every spirit, situation, or person sent by Satan to lull a man of destiny into spiritual sleep. Her lap is an altar where many have sacrificed their anointing.

Throughout history, both kings and commanders have lost nations—not on the battlefield, but in the bedroom. It has been said: *More wars have been lost over a woman than won with a sword.*

From biblical figures like **David,** who compromised with Bathsheba, to modern leaders who fell to temptation disguised as love, the strategy has remained the same—*seduce the leader and weaken the kingdom.*

Wisdom Key: *When Satan cannot defeat a man in combat, he will distract him in comfort.*

The seductive spirit doesn't need to wage war with weapons—it wins through whispers.

It studies your appetite, then sends what looks like relief. That's how kingdoms fall. That's how Samson fell. And that's how many men— preachers, ministers, officers, husbands, prophets—are falling today.

Samson represents every leader, preacher, or prophet who starts strong but finishes broken when discernment is laid aside.

His hair, a symbol of his consecration, becomes the object of betrayal. His fall is a warning to every called man: *What you allow in your heart will eventually touch your head.*

Just as Israel's deliverance was delayed by Samson's downfall, so too can today's revival be delayed by undisciplined vessels. The enemy doesn't need to kill the man—just compromise the mission and the calling.

Delilah's presence in Samson's life is a symbol of how Satan subtly enters sacred spaces through *unchecked desire, emotional neediness,* and *spiritual blindness*. But God gives us the tools to see, to resist, and to stand.

The next chapter will uncover how these spirits enter the lives of strong men—especially those in ministry—and how to discern their presence before it's too late.

Though the name **"Jezebel spirit"** is not directly mentioned in the Bible, its operation is very real.

It is a demonic force characterized by *control, seduction, manipulation, rebellion, and spiritual adultery.* It is sent from Satan himself—designed *to infiltrate, dominate,* and *destroy prophetic order and godly authority.*

The original Jezebel, wife of **King Ahab**, was responsible for silencing the prophets, promoting idolatry, and seducing a nation into corruption.

This same spirit works today—cloaked not in royalty, but in *religion, relationships,* and *even leadership structures.*

The Jezebel spirit operates with precision: *it flatters, seduces, and then enslaves.* Whenever the soul begins to dominate the spirit, a counterfeit authority begins to emerge—and that is the realm where Jezebel thrives.

Spiritual warfare seldom begins with visible attacks—it begins with subtle compromises. The Jezebel spirit is not loud at first—it is calculated. It works in the shadows until it can take the stage.

To deny its reality simply because it isn't named in the New Testament is to ignore the patterns Scripture clearly reveals.

Just as Satan disguises himself as an angel of light, Jezebel comes cloaked in *beauty, charisma, and false spiritual authority.* But her fruit is always the same: *rebellion, idolatry, division, and death.*

Chapter 2 will unmask this spirit further and reveal how it silences prophetic voices and seeks to control those it cannot possess.

Reflective Questions:

1. Have you ever trusted someone with a sacred part of your life, only to be betrayed? What did it cost you spiritually?

2. What are the "Delilah's" in your life today—people or patterns that wear you down emotionally or spiritually?

3. Can you identify moments when emotional fatigue made you more vulnerable to spiritual compromise?

4. Do you know the difference between someone who loves your calling and someone who is assigned to destroy it?

5. Are you protecting the part of your life that holds your spiritual strength, or are you casually exposing it?

Reflective Summary:

Samson's fall was not simply the result of a seductive woman—it was the product of delayed *obedience, emotional weakness, and the failure to discern danger wrapped in beauty.*

Delilah never had love in her heart; she had an agenda. And like many spirits operating today, she gained access through what *felt good, sounded right, and appeared safe.*

The Delilah spirit does not look like a sword—it looks like rest. And by the time it strikes, it's already too late. Every man must take inventory of his vulnerabilities. Strength without discernment is a setup for destruction.

Prayer:

Lord, open my eyes. Show me where I've laid my head in the wrong lap.

Reveal the Delilah's in my life—people, temptations, and spirits sent to destroy the calling You placed on me.

Give me the wisdom to guard what is holy, the courage to walk away from what is deadly, and the power to stand as a man of God, fully armed in discernment and truth.

Let me not fall where others have fallen. Let me rise where others were broken. Let my strength be renewed in Your presence, and my heart be anchored in Your will.

In Jesus' name, Amen.

Chapter 2 — When Control Fails, Jezebel Kills

"A foolish woman is clamorous: she is simple, and knoweth nothing. For she sitteth at the door of her house, on a seat in the high places of the city, To call passengers who go right on their ways."

— Proverbs 9:13–15 (KJV)

There is a spirit that doesn't flirt—it fights. It doesn't seduce—it seizes. And while **Delilah** disarmed Samson through *comfort and flattery,* **Jezebel** wages war through *control, intimidation,* and *manipulation.*

This spirit is not imaginary. Though the phrase *"Jezebel spirit"* isn't found word-for-word in Scripture, its fingerprints are all over the Bible—and still all over the Church today.

It is a demonic weapon of Satan, crafted to *oppose, usurp,* and *silence* prophetic voices, especially in men who carry *authority, discernment,* and *divine assignment.*

Jezebel's original appearance in Scripture is in **1 Kings.** She was the wife of King Ahab, but she never functioned as a wife—she operated as a ruler.

Ahab wore the crown, but Jezebel controlled the decisions. He had the throne; she had the authority. This inversion of divine order was no accident—it was a satanic design.

Wisdom Key: *The Jezebel spirit cannot coexist with divine authority. Where it cannot control, it seeks to destroy.*

A Lived Lesson

Elijah, the prophet of God, stood toe-to-toe with the false prophets Jezebel promoted. He called down fire, exposed corruption, and prayed for rain. But after his greatest spiritual victory, Jezebel sent a single message—not a sword, not an army, just a message—and the prophet of God ran for his life.

This is how Jezebel operates: she doesn't always confront with force; *she works through fear, intimidation, psychological warfare,* and *subtle threats.* She attacks after your highest spiritual moment—because that's when you're tired, exposed, and emotionally drained.

Elijah had just called fire from heaven, yet ran from a woman with no flame at all.

Why?

Because the Jezebel spirit doesn't fight you with weapons—it fights you with weariness. And what it cannot control, it will try to eliminate.

This is not theory. I've lived it.

While stationed overseas, I was called to preach and minister. But even in that sacred assignment, warfare came—not just from external pressure, but through personal entanglement.

I first met Kelly while stationed in Washington, D.C. At the time, I thought she was the best thing that had ever happened to me. One of the subtle lures she used to disarm me was her ability to create an atmosphere of comfort.

I vividly remember how, during my stay in D.C., she would make strawberry shortcakes for me—something I had never had before.

On the surface, it felt harmless and thoughtful. But now I see it for what it was: a calculated way to lower my guard. Seduction doesn't always show up in sensuality; sometimes it's served on a plate with a smile.

These were not gifts of love—they were lures of deception. They created a false sense of peace that numbed my spiritual sensitivity and opened the door to deeper compromise.

When I was assigned to Germany, she eventually followed me there, and we entered into marriage.

At first, she seemed to be an answer to prayer— *attentive, supportive,* and *even spiritually curious.* Despite the clear warning the Lord had given me, I moved forward with the relationship, convinced that I could make it work.

But as time passed, I came to see that God had been right all along. Her true nature slowly began to surface, and what I thought was partnership turned into a battlefield.

The relationship became clouded with *lust, deceit, infidelity, manipulation,* and *emotional instability.*

I was still learning how to be a minister—still finding my voice, understanding the weight of the Word, and discovering what it meant to be called by God.

I was preaching. I was showing up. But inside, I was running on empty. My mouth was declaring truth, but my spirit was gasping for air.

I didn't know how to ask for help, and I didn't realize that my tank had been drained not just by the demands of ministry—but by the quiet warfare that was happening in my home. I was still being formed, still in training, but I was bleeding behind the scenes.

That's how the enemy works—he doesn't wait until you've mastered your anointing. He attacks while you're still learning how to carry it.

I didn't realize it then, but the same spirit that worked through **Delilah** and **Jezebel** was quietly working to wear me down.

What felt like connection was really compromise. What looked like loyalty was spiritual infiltration. That relationship wasn't sent to love me—**she was sent to hinder me.**

I spent years recovering *mentally, financially,* and *socially* from the devastation I experienced while married to her.

Decades later, I reconnected with Jo, my high school sweetheart and the mother of my second child. I thought there might be something redemptive in our reunion, but it only proved to be another lesson.

She had not changed. She had no intention of walking in the Spirit. And once again, my calling was placed in a vulnerable position because of emotional attachment to someone who had no intention of walking in agreement with God's will for my life.

Both situations taught me this: the Jezebel spirit does not always appear through rebellion—it often enters through romance. It wraps itself in familiarity, then begins the slow process of draining discernment.

Translation: *What it cannot possess, it will poison. What it cannot control, it will kill.*

Influence Over Affection

The Jezebel spirit is often cloaked in religious language. It can *sing, dance, preach,* and *prophesy.* It flatters leadership until it can control it. And when that fails, it *assassinates* through *slander, sexual sin, or spiritual fatigue.*

"But I have this against you, that you tolerate that woman Jezebel, who calls herself a prophetess..."

— Revelation 2:20 (KJV)

Jesus didn't condemn Thyatira for letting Jezebel enter—He condemned them for tolerating her.

Tolerance is the trap. She flatters her way into position, then manipulates her way into power.

And when she cannot rise, she works to pull others down.

Wisdom Key: *Jezebel doesn't always want your heart. She wants your influence.*

She wants to stand next to the prophet so she can speak with the prophet's authority. She seduces the anointed so she can control the altar. And if she can't sit on the platform, she'll work the pews until she controls the atmosphere.

Her ultimate assignment?

Assassinate the voice that God raised up to bring truth.

Solomon captured that shameless pattern:

"Such is the way of an adulterous woman; she eateth, and wipeth her mouth, and saith, I have done no wickedness."

— Proverbs 30:20 (KJV)

This proverb exposes the brazenness of sin once conscience is seared: appetite satisfied, traces wiped, innocence declared.

That denial is Jezebel's oxygen—it rebrands manipulation as care and control as counsel until what heaven condemns is calmly tolerated.

She is rarely after affection; she is after authority. If she can stand beside the prophet, she will borrow his voice; if she can't reach the platform, she will shape the pews. **The aim is unchanged:** *silence the truth God sent.*

Wisdom Key: *Jezebel is after your authority, not your affection.*

Recognize the Pattern

- She strikes after spiritual highs, during transitions, or just before a breakthrough.

- She trades affirmation for accountability—praise without push, comfort without correction.

- She reframes manipulation as care, and control as counsel.

- She studies wounds, mirrors desires, and then weaponizes access.

The result is predictable: *the prophet grows weary, prayer thins, boundaries blur, and clarity fades.* Not every "good" connection is a God connection.

Not every reconnection is restoration. Some are recycled assignments of distraction designed to dull discernment.

Peter shows us why some falls happen—not from simple fatigue, but from an uncrucified life that has avoided the cross's training:

"Forasmuch then as Christ hath suffered for us in the flesh, arm yourselves likewise with the same mind: for he that hath suffered in the flesh hath ceased from sin."

— 1 Peter 4:1 (KJV)

Suffering, embraced in Christ, starves the appetites Jezebel exploits. Leaders do not fall because they are merely tired; they fall when comfort becomes their goal and character goes untested.

Trials break *entitlement, fortify conviction, and make compromise costly.*

Wisdom Key: *Suffering isn't a detour—it's armor.*

Guarding the Gates

- **Refuse tolerance.** Confront manipulation wherever it appears—pulpit or pew.

- **Test fruit, not feelings**. Does this relationship sharpen consecration or smother it?

- **Keep order.** Divine authority and accountability are protection, not oppression.

- **Mind the timing.** Guard your soul, especially after victories and during transition.

Reflective Questions:

1. Have you experienced emotional or spiritual manipulation disguised as love or mentorship?

2. In what ways does intimidation or emotional exhaustion silence your prophetic voice?

3. Can you identify people who sought influence in your life without spiritual accountability?

4. Are there areas in your ministry or relationships where control has replaced Holy Ghost-led order?

5. What personal patterns or relationships do you now recognize as spiritually toxic?

Reflective Summary:

The Jezebel spirit doesn't just want to enter your life—it wants to rule.

Its goal is to silence every man and woman who has been called to confront *darkness, deliver truth, and expose idolatry.*

It enters subtly, but it ends in destruction. Whether you are a minister, leader, soldier, or servant, the enemy desires to compromise your calling—not by attacking your strength, but by exploiting your weakness.

Like Samson. Like Elijah. But God has given us the tools *to see, to resist, and to stand.*

Prayer:

Lord, I repent for tolerating anything that opposes Your Spirit.

Expose every Jezebel spirit trying to operate in my life, my home, my church, or my calling.

Break the power of manipulation, seduction, and fear.

Restore my spiritual vision.

Give me strength like Elijah and discipline like Paul.

Let me not be weary in well doing, and let me never mistake control for counsel. Deliver me from deception, and raise me to speak boldly again.

In Jesus' name, Amen.

Chapter 3: When Strength Meets Seduction — The Hidden War for Consecration

"With her much fair speech she caused him to yield, with the flattering of her lips she forced him."

— Proverbs 7:21

There is a point in every man's life — especially the one called by God — when the greatest danger is not the enemy on the battlefield but the invitation in the bedroom.

This is not about lust alone; it is about **access.** When a prophet sleeps, a gate opens. And when that gate is unguarded, hell enters disguised as comfort.

The spirit of the strange woman never rushes. Like Delilah, it studies. It learns a man's fears, frustrations, and — most dangerously — his needs: not only physical, but emotional voids, spiritual hunger, and buried wounds.

That is why so many men in ministry fall: not simply because they are exhausted, but because they fail to discern the patterns of the enemy and the warfare attached to their calling.

Paul warned that we are not to be *ignorant of Satan's devices,* yet countless leaders walk into traps because they are under-developed in spiritual warfare and prematurely released into roles they are not trained to defend. Exhaustion plays a role, but **immaturity magnifies the risk.**

When spiritual discipline weakens, temptation strengthens; when discernment lapses, seduction gains access.

Dealing with Temptation Wisely (The H.A.L.T. Principle)

In his message "Dealing with Temptation Wisely," **Dr. Charles Stanley** offers a practical key to overcoming temptation. He reminds us that most spiritual failures occur not because we are evil, but because we are vulnerable — physically, emotionally, and spiritually. He uses the acronym **H.A.L.T.,** which stands for *Hungry, Angry, Lonely,* and *Tired.*

Dr. Stanley explains that these four conditions are when we are most likely to make poor decisions or yield to temptation. When you are **too hungry**, judgment weakens and the flesh demands to be fed. When you are **too angry,** emotions drown out the still, small voice of God. When you are **too lonely,** companionship may be sought in the wrong place or person. And when you are **too tired**, shortcuts appear reasonable, offering relief that leads only to regret.

The wisdom in this teaching is simple yet profound: *Do not make spiritual decisions when your defenses are down.*

Dr. Stanley urges believers to "stop and **HALT**" before reacting — pause long enough to ask whether one of these four states is shaping your response. The moment you recognize it, invite the Holy Ghost to strengthen your mind, renew your spirit, and help you take the way of escape God has promised **(1 Corinthians 10:13).**

This principle aligns perfectly with Jesus' example in the wilderness. After fasting forty days, He was hungry — and that was when Satan came. The enemy always waits until defenses are low to whisper his loudest lies. But by applying the **H.A.L.T.** principle, we learn to identify weakness before temptation gains control.

The next time you feel drawn toward compromise, stop and **HALT**:

- Are you hungry for something God hasn't given?

- Are you angry about something you haven't released?

- Are you lonely and trying to fill a void only God can fill?

- Are you tired and neglecting the rest your soul needs?

The Holy Ghost will never leave you without a warning. Sometimes He simply whispers, "You need to HALT."

From H.A.L.T. to Holy Ground: The Samson Parallel

Samson's fall did not begin when his hair was cut; it began when he allowed someone without covenant to lie next to his calling. That hair represented more than strength — it represented **consecration,** and consecration is fragile in the wrong company.

The **H.A.L.T.** principle reveals where weakness starts; Samson's story shows how far it can go when ignored.

The hunger for affection, the anger of loneliness, the weariness of constant warfare — all four open the door Delilah waits behind. Spiritual compromise always begins in the small, tired spaces we refuse to guard.

Allegory / Typology: Samson, Delilah, and the Order of the Soul

A called man (Samson) walks in unusual strength because he keeps unusual vows. Over time, the lower nature whispers through "Delilah" — not merely a person but a **pattern** of *comfort, vanity, and impulse* dressed as care.

She never attacks his strength head-on; she bargains away his practices **(the "hair")**: *prayer becomes late, fasting optional, counsel intrusive, secrecy normal.* He naps on affirmation, wakes to emptiness, and learns that the price of relief is power.

Sight goes first (discernment), **then chains** (cycles), then grinding (shame). Yet grace gives a final word: **hair grows** — disciplines can be restored — and yielded weakness can still pull down the idol of self.

Typology Key

- **Samson** → the Spirit-enabled self under call.

- **Hair** → consecration practices and boundaries.

- **Delilah** → *"wisdom from below"* **(James 3:15)** appealing to appetite and ego.

- **Sleep** → spiritual dullness, a numbed conscience.

- **Dagon's fall** → idolatry toppled by surrendered strength.

Call to Action: Guard the hair. Keep the practices that keep the power.

The bedroom of compromise is where many mantles have been lost. This chapter isn't only about physical intimacy; it is about emotional intimacy, spiritual transparency, and sacred vulnerability.

Who do you allow to rest their head near your secrets? Who speaks into your soul when you are weary? Who has access to your cave when you are hiding from the battle?

The Delilah spirit waits until you stop fighting. It doesn't need to force its way in; it waits until you are tired of standing, tired of being alone, tired of praying, tired of always being strong. And when you are most drained, it wraps itself around you — not with war, but with **whispers.**

Wisdom Key: *The greatest battles are not lost in combat — they are lost in comfort.*

Post-Victory Vulnerability

This same pattern appears in Elijah's life. Jezebel didn't confront him on Mount Carmel; she sent a message afterward. Why? Because the prophet was vulnerable. After a great spiritual victory often comes a season of emotional depletion, and that is where the strange woman finds her entrance.

Allegory: Like the Trojan horse, the danger was not the enemy at the gate — it was what was welcomed inside.

Strong men fall when guards drop and wounds remain exposed. These spirits do not appear as devils; they arrive as *comfort, affirmation,* or even as a reward for *"faithful service."* They will tell you what others won't, touch what others can't, and make you feel like a man when ministry has made you feel like a machine.

But the cost is always greater than the comfort. Samson lost his strength. Elijah ran in fear. David went silent for nine months after Bathsheba. And many today walk in spiritual blindness because of one night in Delilah's lap.

The military understands infiltration: an army may appear well-guarded from the outside, but if charm or persuasion gains access to leadership, the whole camp is compromised. The same is true in the spirit.

Churches have been overtaken, ministries aborted, marriages destroyed — not from pulpits but from pews; not from public attack but private alliance. That is why **discernment is not optional — it is essential.**

Wisdom Key: *If the enemy cannot destroy you with force, he will try to access you through familiarity.*

There are women — and yes, men too — sent to derail destiny not by opposing it but by appearing to agree with it. They clap for your sermons, cry at your altar, and declare, *"I'm here to support your vision."* But discernment must rise above emotion. Support is not always divine sanction. Just because someone celebrates your calling does not mean they were sent by God.

Let this be a **divine wake-up call:** watch who speaks into your fatigue, who comforts your wounds, and above all, **guard your consecration.**

Reflective Questions:

1. Who have you allowed into your life during times of emotional exhaustion?

2. Are there relationships in your life that weaken your consecration?

3. Do you feel more spiritually dull or emotionally entangled since certain connections began?

4. Have you misinterpreted comfort as confirmation?

5. What boundaries have you failed to protect in seasons of spiritual fatigue?

Reflective Summary:

When a prophet sleeps, the gates swing open.

This chapter exposes the pattern by which spiritual infiltration happens—not through sudden rebellion, but slow seduction.

Samson's story was written not just to warn, but to prepare. Every man of God must *guard his heart, protect his consecration, and watch over his assignments*—even in moments of emotional depletion.

The devil doesn't always attack with a sword. Sometimes, he attacks with softness. But those who are awake, who are vigilant, who remain filled with the Spirit, will recognize the trap before it takes their strength.

Prayer:

Lord, help me to remain awake. Don't let me surrender my strength for comfort.

Protect my consecration from compromise. Expose every Delilah spirit near my destiny.

Teach me to recognize false comfort and emotional manipulation.

Give me eyes to see when my guard is slipping.

Let my purpose be preserved in purity.

Strengthen me in my moments of weariness, and anchor me in Your truth.

In Jesus' name, Amen.

Chapter 4: How Hell Hushes Prophets

"She hath cast down many wounded: yea, many strong men have been slain by her."

— **Proverbs 7:26**

There is a reason hell sends certain women into the lives of certain men.

It is not always about lust. It is about **legacy.**

It is not always about seduction. It is about **silencing the prophetic voice** before it shakes a generation.

The *strange woman* doesn't target everyone. She is strategic. She seeks out men with **fire in their bones**—men like *Elijah, Jeremiah, and John the Baptist*—men who carry messages that expose false systems and tear down satanic strongholds. Once she identifies that fire, she begins her mission: **not to love it, but to kill it.**

She will affirm you just enough to lower your guard. She will study your rhythm until she knows your weak hour.

She will wait until you're tired—when your prayers grow shallow and your spiritual hunger dulls. Then she will come, disguised as peace, masked in flattery, cloaked in comfort.

She's not after your heart. She's after your **voice.**

Because if she can silence your voice, she can shut down the very move of God that was about to break loose in your life, your church, your family, and your region.

Wisdom Key: *What Satan cannot destroy through fear, he will attempt to destroy through familiarity.*

Delilah didn't look dangerous. Neither did Jezebel at first. But both carried the same mission: silence the man of God before he fulfills what he was born to do.

The Slow Erosion of Strength

In many cases, this silencing begins with a gradual erosion of spiritual strength. It doesn't start with scandal—**it starts with surrendering little convictions.**

- **Prayer** time slowly shortens.

- **Fasting** becomes optional.

- **Accountability** feels intrusive.

- **The Word** no longer convicts—it merely informs.

That's when the enemy knows the gate is unguarded.

This is not just a story about two women in Scripture—it is a **portrait of an ancient assignment.**

Just as Pharaoh issued a decree to kill the male Hebrew children in Moses' day, and Herod did the same in Jesus' day, so too does Satan release targeted attacks against prophetic men today.

The assignment remains unchanged: **kill the deliverer.**

And one of hell's most effective weapons **is the wrong woman.**

The Timing of Temptation

This is why the enemy doesn't send Delilah to the carnal man—he sends her to the **consecrated** one. The one who's been fasting, the one who just came off revival, the one who's preparing to preach, the one who just received a prophetic word.

She comes not only with **temptation,** but with **timing.**

Allegory: *A roaring fire needs oxygen to burn, but all it takes is a blanket of comfort to smother it.*

Sometimes comfort is the most dangerous thing to a prophet.

Many men who once roared like lions now meow like kittens—not because they lost their calling, but because they **laid it down for affection.** They traded their mantle for moments, their vision for validation, their truth for temporary pleasure.

And the result?

A silenced prophet. A dimmed light. A stolen legacy.

Wisdom Key: *Not every kind woman is a kingdom woman.*

The Game: When the Whole Family Plays Along

An associate once revealed to me that often her entire family is part of the game to trap you and to ruin your life —it's a game.

Not just a flirtation or coincidence, but a **coordinated deception** designed to trap the prophetic.

Delilah didn't act alone. She had a covenant with the Philistine lords, who promised her silver for Samson's secret. Jezebel had Ahab's authority and a house full of eunuchs who carried out her schemes. Likewise, in modern times, the "game" often extends beyond the individual—it becomes **a family system**, **a soulish alliance** woven together by **familiar spirits.**

They share information. They exchange strategies. They feign concern. One distracts you; another gathers intelligence. What looks like hospitality is often reconnaissance. The whole household, knowingly or unknowingly, becomes part of a **network of control**—a human web used by the enemy to monitor, manipulate, and mute the prophetic voice.

They laugh together at what they call *"just fun,"* but the Spirit of God calls it **witchcraft in disguise**—soulish influence empowered by demonic suggestion. Their smiles are rehearsed; their questions are bait, their kindness is calculated.

This is the game: to make you believe you are safe in their company while your discernment is slowly being dulled by their attention.

Wisdom Key: *Hell, never plays fair; it plays familiar.*

The game is ancient. **Eve** played it with the serpent in Eden, exchanging revelation for conversation. Delilah played it for profit. Jezebel played it for power. Today, families play it for pride, protection, or pleasure—rarely realizing they are serving the same agenda: **to neutralize the prophetic before it exposes their system.**

This is why you must test **not just the individual, but the entire circle.** If her family mocks your faith, disrespects your calling, or subtly challenges your convictions, understand: the same spirit operating in her may have already found a home in them.

Allegory: *The strange woman is never alone—she travels with a network. The bait is personal, but the trap is collective.*

When you sense that every conversation ends with confusion, every visit leaves you drained, and every connection feels like surveillance, you are no longer dealing with coincidence—you are confronting **coordination.**

Prophetic men must recognize that hell doesn't send random attacks; it sends **assignments.** When the enemy cannot strike you openly, he will surround you quietly. The game is not about romance—it's about reconnaissance. The goal is not affection—it's information.

And once they know what keeps you strong, they work together to separate you from it.

Recognizing the Web

- Does the conversation always circle back to your weakness?

- Do "friends" seem unusually aware of your private details?

- Do you sense manipulation disguised as concern?

These are signs the game has begun.

Like Nehemiah's enemies who conspired in secret to lure him off the wall, the purpose of the game is always the same: **to stop the building.** Stop the prayer life. Stop the prophetic flow.

Stop the voice that threatens the kingdom of darkness.

Wisdom Key: *Where manipulation multiplies, revelation dies.*

That is why prophetic men must be vigilant—not only about their personal holiness, but about the circles they keep. If she doesn't respect your prayer life, she's not your helpmate. If her family mocks your calling, they are not your allies. If she wants your affection more than your obedience to God—**run.**

Because once your voice is gone, so is your edge. Your vision. Your discernment. Your mantle.

The Final Warning

Let this chapter serve as both **a warning and a wake-up call.**

God is not just raising up strong voices; He is raising up discerning spirits—men and women who can recognize when comfort is camouflage and when charm is a chain.

Hell's game is still the same: silence the prophets before they speak, distract them before they discern, and seduce them before they stand.

But Heaven's call remains stronger: *be sober, be vigilant, for your adversary the devil walketh about, seeking whom he may devour* **(1 Peter 5:8).**

So stay sober.

Stay watchful.

Stay prophetic.

Reflective Questions:

1. What warning signs did Samson overlook in Delilah's behavior, and are there any similar red flags present in your own relationships?

2. Has your voice grown quiet in the Spirit? Could compromise or distraction be part of the cause?

3. In what ways has comfort become more important to you than consecration?

4. Have you mistaken flattery or emotional support for godly confirmation?

5. Who in your life truly strengthens your anointing—and who slowly weakens it?

Reflective Summary:

In this chapter, we uncover the chilling reality of spiritual assassination—not by swords, but by seduction.

The Strange Woman does not come to the prophet as a loud enemy, but as a silent friend.

Her goal is not just to seduce the man, but to silence the voice God gave him. Her weapons are flattery, comfort, and carefully timed affection— all designed to lull the prophet to sleep just before his greatest assignment.

The tragedy isn't always in the fall—it's in the forfeiture of voice, vision, and consecration.

Many anointed men have lost their spiritual edge not through sin that came quickly, but through compromise that came softly. This spirit is subtle. It studies the strong. And it shows up not during rebellion, but during weariness.

Chapter 4 sounds the alarm that prophets must not only speak boldly—they must guard carefully. Because the enemy isn't just after your heart… he's after your sound. Your authority. Your fire. Your ability to disturb hell and awaken heaven.

Prayer:

Father, in the name of Jesus, I come before You, asking for divine wisdom and holy fire. Lord, open my eyes to every spirit sent to silence my voice, dull my discernment, and derail my destiny. Expose the Delilahs. Unmask the Jezebels. Reveal the motives of every false assignment.

Where I have been tired, refresh me. Where I have been numb, revive me. Where I have compromised, forgive me—and restore my strength.

Teach me to treasure my calling, guard my purity, and protect my voice. May I be found faithful. May I be found watchful. And may I never exchange my mantle for a moment of pleasure.

In Jesus' mighty name, Amen.

Chapter 5: The Spirit That Sedates Prophets

Preface

In the last chapter, we saw how hell hushes prophets through deception.

But when the enemy cannot silence a voice outright, he chooses a subtler tactic—**to sedate it.**

The devil doesn't always come with war; sometimes he comes with warmth. He rocks the prophet to sleep with comfort, compliments, and convenience until fire becomes flicker and discernment becomes drowsiness.

Let us now look deeper into the slow and silent death that overtakes a prophet who stops guarding his gates.

"Her feet go down to death; her steps take hold on hell."

— Proverbs 5:5

There is a danger more deadly than the sword. More subtle than poison. More powerful than fear.

It is the gradual dulling of a man's spiritual sensitivity.

The enemy rarely attacks the anointing head-on. Instead, he sends something soft—something that looks safe. Something that wraps itself around the prophet like a warm blanket and slowly suffocates his discernment.

Discernment doesn't die all at once.

It dies in stages.

It begins with one conversation too long. One hug too tight. One compliment too sweet. One prayer missed. One boundary overlooked.

And suddenly, the man who once had sharp vision now walks blindly into the lap of Delilah.

Discernment Declines When Desire Rises

Samson didn't lose his strength first; he lost his sight.

He began desiring what he should have been resisting. That is the mark of a man under seduction—he longs for what he used to pray against.

A man cannot walk in discernment and delusion at the same time.

The strange woman doesn't just lure the flesh—she dulls the spirit. She numbs the prophet until he no longer knows what's from God and what's from hell.

He may still quote Scripture. He may still attend church. But inside, the flame flickers.

She doesn't kill with a dagger—she drains with distraction.

Wisdom Key: *Seduction rarely starts with sin; it starts with sympathy for what you should rebuke.*

Special Note (Doctrinal Framework)

Flesh vs. **Spirit** — A Cosmology of the Lower Nature

Before we go deeper, let's anchor this warfare in doctrine. Scripture reveals a real conflict in the human person: **the flesh** (lower nature) versus **the Spirit.**

To *"think with the lower nature"* is to let appetites, fear, vanity, and impulse steer the mind instead of reason, conscience, and the Holy Ghost **(Rom 8:5, 8; Gal 5:16, 25).**

James contrasts two wisdoms—one earthly, sensual, devilish that breeds envy and disorder, and one from above that yields purity and peace **(Jas 3:15, 17).**

Key Discernment: *The source determines the fruit.*

What begins in flesh ends in bondage; what begins in Spirit ends in freedom.

The Strange Woman as Lower-Nature "Wisdom"

Proverbs paint the strange woman as strategic appetite—*flattering speech, staged secrecy,* and *timing that exploits fatigue.* She markets the lower nature: permission without purity, pleasure without consequence, intimacy without covenant. That is **James 3:15** in a dress—*earthly, sensual, devilish.*

• **Her logic:** "If it soothes you now, it must be good."

• **Her fruit:** envy, confusion, and disorder—first in the soul, then in the house, then in the church.

• **Her aim:** separate a man from the conditions of his strength—consecration, obedience, accountability—then sell him to his enemies.

Wisdom Key: *The lower nature always sounds reasonable when you're tired; the Spirit remains righteous when you are.*

Why Some Preachers Fall: The Cross They Avoided (1 Peter 4)

"Forasmuch then as Christ hath suffered for us in the flesh, arm yourselves likewise with the same mind: for he that hath suffered in the flesh hath ceased from sin." — **1 Peter 4:1**

"Suffering in the flesh" is training—the cruciform schooling that starves the appetites the strange woman manipulates. Where leaders skip the cross, three vulnerabilities grow:

• **Unbroken appetite** (comfort becomes the goal),

• **Thin endurance** (weariness drives decisions),

• **Cheap discernment** (peace is confused with relief).

Result: a preacher may preach truth publicly while privately negotiating with the lower nature.

Without the cross, Delilah's lap feels like rest; with the cross, it reads like risk.

Wisdom Key: *Trials don't make you holy; they remove what keeps you from holiness.*

Guardrails for Leaders

• **Train the appetite** (fasting, simplicity, curfew on screens & DMs).

• **Tend the mind** (daily Word; three Scriptures against your three most common pulls).

• **Tighten the circle** (two-person rule; no closed-door private counsel with emotionally attached women).

• **Tell the truth early** (bring temptation to light before it grows).

• **Take the cross seriously** (scheduled fasts; accept hard providences as training, **1 Pet 4:1-2**).

Wisdom Key: *If it requires a lie to live, it did not come from Light.*

The Watchman and the Sedative (Allegory)

Picture a powerful watchman standing on a tower—eyes sharp, sword ready. Then someone hands him a warm drink and invites him to rest. *"Just a short break,"* they say. The wind is cool. The blanket is soft. And the sedative begins to work.

That sedative is compromise. That warm drink is flattery. That blanket is unholy affection.

And by the time he wakes up, the city is overrun, and his weapon is gone.

Familiarity — Satan's Favorite Entry Point

Satan will never tempt you with what feels evil; he tempts you with what feels familiar.

It may be her *kindness,* her ability *to listen*, her *support of your ministry*, her soft words when you feel *misunderstood.* But if her presence pulls you away from God instead of toward Him—it is not comfort; it is a trap.

Wisdom Key: *If she cannot stir your spirit, she has no business holding your heart.*

The death of discernment comes not because the man is evil—but because he did not recognize what he carried. Without revelation of the anointing's worth, he becomes vulnerable—not only to temptation but to manipulation and comfort that erodes his edge.

The Exhaustion Factor

Men in ministry often fall not from pride but from fatigue. Exhaustion breeds vulnerability; if left unchecked, discernment grows dull.

Satan doesn't just attack strength—he waits until you are spiritually dehydrated.

That's why the strange woman always appears:

- After a spiritual high,

- During transition,

- Right before promotion,

- Just before breakthrough.

Because the enemy knows: if he can reach you in-between, he can intercept the call.

Personal Application (Drawn from Faith and Fire)

Jo knew, I assumed, how much I loved her. When we reunited in 2007 after twenty-four years apart, I believed the connection was ordained. Though the Lord once told me I would never see her again, emotion overrode instruction.

Her presence made me feel invincible, as if the pain of the past had finally found peace. But her comfort was not covenant—**it was strategy**.

When I explained that we would not engage in sex, she agreed—then demanded it. I tried to resist, even sought another room, but the hotel was full. Satan had arranged the details.

We sinned that day. It was not thrilling—it was hollow. What I wanted was communion of spirit; what I received was the counterfeit of flesh.

We married in 2008 and remained nearly ten years. She never honored me as a husband or a man of God.

In 2018, we divorced—and she left with half my windfall. What I mistook for love was a costly distraction.

Her gestures felt soothing but were spiritually disarming. Each indulgence dulled my edge until the prophet in me was tired, not dead—but sedated.

Final Admonition

Discernment dies when a man stops guarding his gates. *Your eyes, your ears, your heart—*they are sacred.

What you allow in will either protect your destiny or pollute it.

What feels good now may cost you your calling later.

Wisdom Key: *The Spirit revives what the flesh ruins—but only when the man awakens.*

Reflective Questions:

1. Where have I allowed my spiritual discernment to grow dull, and why?

2. Are there voices or relationships in my life that feel comforting but are spiritually draining?

3. What patterns have I ignored that suggest I'm slowly compromising?

4. Am I mistaking kindness or attention for spiritual alignment?

5. What boundaries must I restore to protect the fire of my calling?

Reflective Summary:

Discernment does not die with a bang—it fades with a whisper. This chapter reveals how the enemy seldom attacks the man of God with violence, but with comfort. It is not always the obvious sin that destroys a calling—it is the slow, steady erosion of spiritual sharpness through unchecked emotion, unguarded affection, and unrepented compromise.

Samson didn't fall because of Delilah's strength—he fell because of his own spiritual fatigue and emotional vulnerability. And like so many today, he mistook kindness for alignment, and comfort for confirmation. The Strange Woman didn't have to kill him—she only had to lull him to sleep.

This chapter forces the reader to examine the gradual steps that lead to spiritual dullness: missed prayer, ignored conviction, overlooked boundaries. The cost of letting down your guard is not only delay—it can be destiny lost.

But hope remains. Discernment can be restored. The fire can burn again. If the man of God will return to the altar, restore his gates, and reject every comfort that costs him his clarity, he can walk again in full spiritual authority.

Prayer:

Father, in the name of Jesus, restore my discernment. Let every scale fall from my eyes.

Show me the doors I've left open, and help me close them with conviction. Strengthen me in the secret place until I can once again hear Your voice clearly and respond with obedience.

I rebuke the spirit of slumber, deception, and emotional manipulation. I will not be lulled to sleep by comfort. I will not be seduced by flattery. I will not sacrifice my future for false peace.

Awaken me, O God. Reignite the fire. Sharpen my vision. And let me walk with boldness, purity, and power.

In Jesus' name, Amen.

Special Note Before Chapter 6: Clarifying the Terminology

Before we move deeper into the spiritual tactics behind these seductive forces, it is essential that we define the three primary terms referenced throughout this book: **the Strange Woman, the Whorish Woman, the Adulterous Woman,** this list also includes **the Evil Woman, the Foolish Woman and the Contentious/Brawling/Angry Woman.**

These are not interchangeable phrases—they carry unique spiritual characteristics, although they often work together to undermine the life of a man of God.

Warning: These are women a man of God should avoid at all cost.

The Strange Woman

The Bible repeatedly warns about the Strange
Woman, particularly in Proverbs (see **Proverbs
2:16, 5:3, 6:24, 7:5**, and others). She is not
merely unfamiliar; she is foreign to the covenant
of God. *She doesn't honor spiritual order, divine
purpose, or holy living.*

She appears pleasant, even harmless—but her
agenda is aligned with hell. She seeks the
vulnerable, the tired, the called—and she hunts
"for the precious life."

Key Traits:

- Smooth, flattering speech that disarms discernment **(Prov 2:16; 5:3; 7:21).**

- Uses appearance and allure ("attire of an harlot") to entice **(Prov 7:10).**

- Loud, stubborn; feet do not abide at home **(Prov 7:11).**

- Lies in wait; bold face; catches and kisses **(Prov 7:12–13).**

- Cloaks seduction in religious language ("peace offerings… vows have I paid") to appear safe **(Prov 7:14).**

- Creates sensual atmosphere (perfumed bed, colored linens) to lower resistance **(Prov 7:16–17).**

- Downplays consequences ("the goodman is not at home") to quiet conscience **(Prov 7:19–20).**

- Her path leads to death; has cast down many strong men **(Prov 7:26–27).**

The Whorish Woman

A KJV term used to warn about the destructive power of sexual immorality and its predatory, impoverishing effect on men and households **(Prov 6:26; 23:27; 29:3; cf. Hos 4:11).**

Key Traits:

- Reduces a man to "a piece of bread" — material and moral depletion **(Prov 6:26).**

- Hunts for the precious life; predatory intent **(Prov 6:26).**

- Is like a deep ditch and a narrow pit —
  dangerous and hard to escape **(Prov
  23:27).**

- Association leads to waste and shame;
  *"he… that keepeth company with harlots
  spendeth his substance"* **(Prov 29:3).**

- Entices with visible signals and bold
  approach (attire of an harlot; subtle of
  heart) **(Prov 7:10).**

- "Whoredom… taketh away the heart" —
  dulls discernment and enslaves desire **(Hos
  4:11).**

The Adulterous Woman

The adulterous woman is one who violates covenant. Her sin is not only one of the flesh but of betrayal.

She seeks what is not hers and destroys what was meant to be sacred.

In Scripture, adultery is not only a physical act but also symbolic of spiritual unfaithfulness.

This type of woman may seduce a man away from his commitment—whether to a spouse, a calling, or to God Himself. She is reckless with boundaries and dangerous to destinies.

Key Traits:

- Forsakes covenant: leaves the guide of her youth and forgets the covenant of her God **(Prov 2:17).**

- Self-justifying denial: *"she eateth, and wipeth her mouth, and saith, I have done no wickedness"* **(Prov 30:20).**

- Lures to illicit intimacy with persuasive words and promise of secret pleasure **(Prov 7:18).**

- Deceptive timing and cover: *"the goodman is not at home... he will come at the day appointed"* **(Prov 7:19–20).**

- **Consequences for the man:** *"destroyeth his own soul… a wound and dishonour… reproach shall not be wiped away"* **(Prov 6:32–33).**

- Provokes the husband's jealousy and vengeance; no gift can appease **(Prov 6:34–35).**

- Her house inclines unto death; none that go to her return **(Prov 2:18–19).**

The Evil Woman

Named explicitly in **Proverbs 6:24**—often paired with the *"strange woman."* Her tool is flattery; her aim is capture. See also the consequence language surrounding sexual folly **(Prov 6:26).**

Key Traits:

- Flattering tongue; manipulative words **(Prov 6:24).**

- Seductive looks—"eyelids"—that ensnare the heart **(Prov 6:25).**

- Reduces a man to a "piece of bread" through lust and loss **(Prov 6:26).**

- Hunts for the precious life; predatory intent **(Prov 6:26).**

The Foolish Woman

Described as clamorous, simple, and undiscerning—her influence destroys wisdom and invites death **(Prov 9:13; cf. 14:1 for contrast with the wise woman).**

Key Traits:

- Noisy, undiscerning; lacks knowledge **(Prov 9:13).**

- Publicly positions herself to lure the unwary (sits at doors/high places) **(Prov 9:14–15).**

- Sells secrecy and stolen pleasure ("stolen waters are sweet") **(Prov 9:17).**

- Blind to the mortal end of her house; her guests are in the depths of hell **(Prov 9:18).**

- Tears down her own house by folly **(Prov 14:1, negative contrast).**

The Contentious / Brawling / Angry Woman

A profile marked by strife, quarrelsomeness, and relentless agitation that erodes the peace of a home and community **(Prov 21:9, 21:19; 25:24; 27:15–16).**

Key Traits:

- Provokes continual conflict; living with her is compared to a rooftop corner or wilderness **(Prov 21:9, 21:19; 25:24).**

- Like a continual dripping on a rainy day— wearisome and unrelenting **(Prov 27:15).**

- Difficult to restrain or reason with **(Prov 27:16).**

Her Cunning (Subtilty & Strategy)

Scripture does not present the strange/adulterous/whorish woman as merely sensual but strategic—subtil **(Gen 3:1),** operating with premeditation and deception **(2 Cor 11:3).**

She studies, scouts, and stages the moment **(Prov 7:10–21);** she hunts for the precious life **(Prov 6:26);** she manufactures the illusion of safety (perfume, linens, secrecy, timing) to seduce the undiscerning **(Prov 7:16–20).**

She does not live by God's covenantal standards—she forgets the covenant of her God **(Prov 2:17)**—and then self-justifies her actions: *"I have done no wickedness"* **(Prov 30:20).**

In modern terms: she often moves ten steps ahead of a tired or unguarded man—reading his needs, forging alibis, and co-opting religious language to mute his alarms **(Prov 7:14, 21)**.

This is especially evident in matters of finances and secret affairs. *Yet the Lord disappointeth the devices of the crafty* **(Job 5:12).**

Financial Cunning: Extraction & Ensnarement

- **Resource drain & dependency:** *"For by means of a whorish woman a man is brought to a piece of bread"*—she reduces strength, savings, and standing **(Prov 6:26; cf. 29:3).**

- **Manufactured urgency:** crises and deadlines become levers *for gifts, loans, and "investments"* **(application of Prov 7:14–20's staging).**

- **Debt entanglements & surety:** she pressures for co-signing, shared bills, and risky pledges—*"he that is surety for a stranger shall smart for it"* **(Prov 6:1–5; 11:15; 17:18).**

- **Opaque money paths:** secrecy around accounts, passwords, and spending; the wise store, the foolish "spendeth it up" **(Prov 21:20).**

- **Leveraging flattery for access:** persuasive words open wallets as easily as they open doors **(Prov 7:21; 5:3).**

Secrecy & Affairs: The Hidden Network

- **Plausible deniability:** *"she... wipeth her mouth, and saith, I have done no wickedness"* **(Prov 30:20).**

- **Timing the secrecy:** *"the goodman is not at home... he will come at the day appointed"*—affairs are scheduled for invisibility **(Prov 7:19–20).**

- **Religious cover:** *"peace offerings... vows have I paid"*—piety is used to sanitize sin **(Prov 7:14).**

- **Predatory spread:** she *"lieth in wait as for a prey, and increaseth the transgressors among men"* **(Prov 23:28; cf. 23:27).**

- **Modern patterns (application):** compartmentalized contacts, "business" pretexts, privacy locks, shadow socials, and selective visibility.

Guardrails for Men of God (Financial & Moral)

- **Keep your heart above all (Prov 4:23);** remove thy way far from her **(Prov 5:8).**

- **Refuse secrecy:** *"have no fellowship with the unfruitful works of darkness, but rather reprove them"* **(Eph 5:11).**

- **No private loans, no co-signing, no shared accounts outside covenant;** flee surety **(Prov 6:1–5; 11:15; 17:18).**

- **Accountability in money and meetings:** *prudent men foresee evil and hide themselves* **(Prov 22:3; 27:12);** walk with the wise **(Prov 13:20).**

- **Make no provision for the flesh**—set practical boundaries for proximity, privacy, and digital access **(Rom 13:14).**

WHY THIS MATTERS

These are behavioral and spiritual profiles—not blanket condemnations of women. Scripture also celebrates <u>the virtuous woman</u> **(Prov. 31)** and the <u>wise woman who builds her house</u> **(Prov. 14:1).**

Our aim is to expose destructive patterns so that men of God—and the Church—*may watch, pray, and walk wisely.*

These spirits don't always present as "evil." They often appear *nurturing, attractive, or even spiritually mature.*

Therefore, the man of God must see beyond appearance. These spirits are masters of camouflage—deployed by the enemy to divert, delay, and ultimately destroy the call of God on a man's life.

Moving forward into **Chapter 6,** we will begin to expose how these women and spirits enter a man's life, how to discern them early, and how to protect your calling from the traps that have destroyed many.

Wisdom Key: *What you cannot define, you cannot discern. And what you do not discern, may one day destroy you.*

Chapter 6: How Hell Gets in the House

"To deliver thee from the strange woman, even from the stranger which flattereth with her words; which forsaketh the guide of her youth, and forgetteth the covenant of her God."

— Proverbs 2:16–17

Hell never storms the gate—it waits for an invitation.

The enemy studies a man of God long before he ever strikes. *He observes his patterns, his vulnerabilities, his emotions, and his appetites.* He knows that the easiest way into a strong man's house is not through force, but through *familiarity.*

Every spirit—whether **the Strange Woman, the Whorish Woman, the Adulterous Woman, the Evil Woman, the Foolish Woman, or the Contentious Woman**—operates with a single purpose: to find an open door.

These spirits do not come kicking and screaming; they come smiling and sympathizing. They arrive not as threats but as **answers**—*to comfort, admiration, or companionship.* But every counterfeit comfort carries a cost.

They enter through unguarded gates: *fatigue, pride, lust, loneliness, rebellion, or emotional hunger.*

No man falls overnight. Before Samson ever lost his hair, he lost his boundaries. Before David ever fell with Bathsheba, he fell asleep on his post. Before Solomon ever built altars to foreign gods, he let his affection wander where his discernment once stood guard.

Hell gains entry one compromise at a time.

The Entry Points of the Enemy

The Strange Woman comes when you are tired of routine. She flatters with novelty and appeals to your ego.

The Whorish Woman comes when your flesh is unattended. She offers thrill in exchange for peace.

The Adulterous Woman comes when covenant feels heavy. She calls rebellion *"freedom"* and deception *"love."*

The Evil Woman comes when bitterness festers and boundaries fall. She makes partnership with darkness seem necessary.

The Foolish Woman comes when correction is ignored. Loud and confident, she offers "stolen waters" that taste sweet and end in death.

The Contentious Woman comes when pride rules the tongue. She turns every conversation into combat until your peace leaks like a slow drip from a broken vessel.

Though their faces differ, their pattern is the same:

- First, they gain your ear.

- Then, they reach your emotions.

- Finally, they take your heart.

Once they have your heart, they have your discernment.

And when discernment is gone, destiny stands in danger.

The Subtle Nature of Infiltration

The devil doesn't need to knock down your door when you leave it cracked with loneliness.

He doesn't need to shout when your heart is hungry for attention.

He will send someone who *sounds like understanding, looks like comfort, and feels like peace.* But the peace of hell is only anesthesia before surgery—it numbs you long enough to steal without resistance.

We imagine the enemy with horns, but more often, he comes with *eyelashes, perfume*, and *perfect timing.*

He knows when your spirit is weary and your emotions are open.

He knows when your prayers have become routine and your hunger has become human.

He waits for you to say, "I just need somebody to talk to."

That is when infiltration begins.

Wisdom Key: *The enemy cannot enter where the Spirit is still invited.*

How the House Becomes Vulnerable

Every man of God builds a spiritual house—made of *prayer, purity, and perseverance*. But even the strongest house can be compromised if the gatekeeper becomes distracted.

Men in ministry are especially vulnerable because of constant emotional output. You *pour, preach, comfort, and counsel*—but if you are never **refilled**, you begin living off emotional fumes. And an empty vessel is a target for demonic occupation.

Dryness breeds distortion. What feels like empathy may be enticement. What feels like rest may be retreat from obedience.

When you are spiritually dry, even Delilah looks like deliverance.

Wisdom Key: *A tired prophet will mistake affection for assignment.*

That's why spiritual maintenance is not optional—it is survival.

When your platform grows faster than your private altar, the cracks form silently. **Prayer** becomes performance. **Conviction** becomes convenience. **Accountability** feels intrusive.

And before long, the door swings open—and hell walks in politely.

Guarding the Gates

If hell gets in through the door, it's because heaven wasn't watching the hinges.

To keep your spiritual house secure:

- **Guard your conversations.** Some words are too sacred for casual ears.

- **Examine your emotional needs.** Not every void need company—some need crucifixion.

- **Surround yourself with accountability.** A man without counsel is a soldier without armor.

- **Stay sensitive to the Holy Ghost.** When He warns, obey. When He convicts, repent. When He pulls, pause.

Discernment is your lock; obedience is your key. Lose either, and the door opens from the inside.

The Pattern of Delilah

Delilah never rushed Samson—she studied him.

She didn't cut his hair on the first night; she comforted him into carelessness. She listened, she soothed, and she asked just the right questions.

Every lap of compromise begins as a pillow of comfort.

Her power was not in scissors—it was in *strategy.* She turned affection into interrogation until Samson surrendered his secret.

She didn't need to overpower him. She waited for him to lower his own walls.

That is how hell works. It doesn't invade—it *infiltrates.* It doesn't break in—it's let in.

Wisdom Key: *Hell never forces entry; it finds agreement.*

The God Who Exposes

Even when deception has slipped in, God remains faithful.

The Spirit of Truth never leaves a man of prayer without a warning. He will tug at your spirit, stir your rest, or use a sermon, a Scripture, or even a stranger to say, "Watch the door."

- If you listen, you will be delivered.

- If you obey, you will be restored.

Every closed door is protection, not punishment.

Every denied connection is deliverance disguised as rejection.

When God closes a door, it's not because He's keeping you from pleasure—He's keeping you from prison.

Closing Admonition

Prophets, preachers, and men of God—guard your house.

The enemy's access point is rarely the front door. It's the side window of **exhaustion.** It's the back porch of **pride.** It's the crack in the wall called **loneliness.**

Tend to your spirit as carefully as you tend to your sermons.

Keep the oil flowing. Keep the altar burning. Keep your heart locked to everything that doesn't lead you closer to Christ.

Because hell can only enter where heaven's presence has been neglected.

Wisdom Key: *Satan's greatest entrances are built on yesterday's unguarded exits.*

Every open door eventually invites a visitor. But not every visitor is meant to stay. Some come to distract, others to dwell—and a few to disguise themselves as destiny.

When hell enters the house, its next move is to build a bedroom. And once the prophet confuses affection for agreement, the trap is no longer at the door—it's at the altar.

That's where the next chapter begins—where emotional need meets spiritual deception, and the man of God becomes tied, but not joined.

Reflective Questions:

1. What "doors" in your life might the enemy be studying right now?

   (Are you guarding your heart, emotions, and private moments with the same vigilance that you guard your public ministry?)

2. Can you identify a time when weariness, loneliness, or pride made you vulnerable to the wrong voice?

   (What did that experience teach you about the importance of resting in God rather than reaching for relief?)

3. Which of the six women—Strange, Whorish, Adulterous, Evil, Foolish, or Contentious—have you most encountered in your spiritual journey?

   (How did the Holy Ghost warn you, and how did you respond?)

4. Are there conversations, relationships, or habits you've allowed that may be giving hell legal access to your spiritual house?

   (What boundaries need to be rebuilt before those openings become entry points?)

5. How can you keep your spiritual house filled with the presence of God so there's no vacancy for deception?

(What consistent disciplines—prayer, fasting, fellowship, or rest—will help you stay alert and protected?)

Reflective Summary:

Every man of God must recognize that hell's entry point is never random—it's relational. The enemy studies your tendencies, learns your triggers, and waits for your weakest moment to disguise temptation as tenderness. He doesn't need the front door when fatigue, loneliness, or pride will leave the side gate open.

This chapter reminds us that spiritual invasion begins with emotional permission. Satan gains access not by force, but by familiarity. He waits for you to confuse comfort with covenant, kindness with calling, and sympathy with Spirit.

The key to survival is not more power—it's more awareness.

To guard your house means to guard your **heart,** your **habits,** and your **hidden places**. It means watching your words, testing your emotions, and maintaining spiritual maintenance through prayer, fasting, and accountability.

If hell has found its way into any room of your life, the mercy of God is still your key of eviction. Close the doors through repentance. Rebuild your altar through prayer. Reinforce your walls through the Word. And remember:

Wisdom Key: *Hell cannot inhabit what holiness continually inspects.*

Prayer:

Lord, open my eyes to see what I have not seen. Reveal the motives behind the words, the spirits behind the smiles, and the agendas behind the affection.

Strengthen me to shut every open door that gives access to the enemy.

Help me to walk in spiritual discernment and not emotional impulse.

Guard my calling, protect my soul, and teach me to value what is holy.

In Jesus' name, Amen.

Chapter 7: Tied but Not Joined - The Cost of a Counterfeit Covenant

"Can two walk together, except they be agreed?"

— **Amos 3:3**

The Illusion of Agreement

Every false covenant begins with a true desire.

The longing to be seen, loved, and understood is not evil—but when it's unmet, it becomes exploitable. That's how many men of God find themselves tied to someone God never joined them to.

Hell knows how to imitate holiness. The enemy will send a person who *sounds spiritual, acts supportive, and appears safe*—until the connection deepens beyond God's boundaries. Suddenly the tie that felt divine becomes a chain that constrains.

A counterfeit covenant is any bond that feels right to the flesh but wars against your purpose. It speaks in the language of love but operates in the logic of loss.

The Difference Between Tying and Joining

- God joins through covenant.

- Satan ties through convenience.

When God joins two lives, the union *multiplies destiny.* When Satan ties two souls, the connection *magnifies distraction.*

To be **joined** is to be *one in spirit*—rooted in shared obedience to the Word of God.

To be **tied** is to be *one in struggle*—bound by emotion, lust, fear, or unhealed need.

You can be legally married and spiritually mismatched.

You can share a bed yet not share a vision.

You can live under one roof and still serve two masters.

The Counterfeit Covenant Pattern

False covenant follows a predictable pattern:

1. Attraction without alignment.

   The bond begins in the realm of emotion
   rather than revelation.

2. Agreement without assignment.

   You both want companionship but not
   necessarily the same calling.

3. Affection without accountability.

   Boundaries dissolve because the
   relationship feeds ego rather than spirit.

4. Alliance without an altar.

   Prayer disappears, and passion becomes
   the only proof of "connection."

By the time the man realizes it, **he is tied but not joined**—spiritually drained yet emotionally dependent.

Allegory: The Silken Cord

Picture a warrior waking from battle, weary but victorious. A woman enters his tent with gentle words and a silken cord. *"Rest,"* she says. *"You've earned it."* He doesn't notice that the cord, soft at first, loops twice, then three times. Each turn feels comforting—until he tries to stand and finds his hands bound.

That silken cord is the counterfeit covenant—smooth, soothing, and strong.

Wisdom Key: *Not every comfort is covenant, and not every connection is covering.*

Why Prophets Are Targeted

The prophetic man carries what hell fears most: **a voice that breaks patterns.** So, the enemy sends relationships designed to dull discernment.

He won't tempt you with open rebellion; he'll tempt you with romance that excuses disobedience. He'll give you someone who celebrates your anointing but undermines your altar.

That's why discernment must test *who celebrates you* and *why.*

Spiritual Law: Unequal Yoking

Paul warned, *"Be not unequally yoked together with unbelievers"* **(2 Cor 6:14).** But unequal yokes aren't limited to faith versus unbelief—they include any partnership where **purpose** is mismatched.

If one partner pursues destiny while the other pursues distraction, the yoke becomes painful.

You cannot walk in divine direction while dragging human delay.

Wisdom Key: *Agreement without assignment becomes entanglement.*

Emotional Dependency vs. Spiritual Intimacy

A true covenant nourishes your spirit; a counterfeit feeds your insecurity.

It keeps you addicted to attention instead of anchored in affection.

That's why many mistake attachment for anointing. They confuse chemistry for confirmation.

But God never called you to be completed by another human; He called you to be complemented by a partner who strengthens your consecration.

Doctrinal Note: Covenant and Consecration

In Scripture, covenant always involves sacrifice. Abraham's covenant required an altar. Christ's covenant required a cross. But counterfeit covenants require neither—they promise union without dying to self.

That's why they fail.

They start in excitement but end in exhaustion.

Wisdom Key: *Any relationship that costs you your peace was too expensive to keep.*

Practical Discernment Checklist

1. Before you call it covenant, test it by these questions:

2. Does this relationship increase or decrease your sensitivity to the Holy Ghost?

3. Does it strengthen your prayer life or substitute for it?

4. Does it bring clarity or confusion?

5. Do you feel covered or controlled?

6. Would you still be in this connection if it required the cross?

Personal Reflection and Warning

Every prophet who lost power did so after trusting the wrong lap. Samson lost his hair. Solomon lost his wisdom. Many modern leaders lose their integrity—not because they stopped loving God, but because they started loving someone who didn't love God's order.

Hell rejoices when holy men marry unhealed women, because the union multiplies dysfunction.

But heaven restores those who repent and return to alignment.

Restoration and Freedom

Being *"tied"* is not the end of your story. God can untie what emotion entangled. He can redeem wasted years and reset wounded hearts. **The key is surrender.**

Ask the Holy Ghost to reveal every ungodly soul-tie. Renounce what was not ordained. Replace manipulation with meditation. Let the Spirit sever what sentiment sustained.

Because once the tie is broken, the joining can begin—*God's way, in God's time, with God's peace.*

Wisdom Key: *Heaven only blesses what heaven begins.*

Transition to Chapter 8

Every false tie leaves a residue. Even after the bond is broken, the echo of that connection tries to linger—*through memories, guilt, or emotional fatigue.* But the same God who exposes deception also **empowers deliverance.**

Breaking free is more than walking away; it's learning to rebuild what hell tried to dismantle—*your confidence, your consecration, and your clarity.*

The next chapter moves from bondage to breakthrough, revealing how the Spirit of God restores the man who was wounded by love but redeemed by truth.

When the tie is broken, the training begins.

Reflective Questions:

1. Have I confused emotional attachment with godly connection?

   (Am I drawn by covenant or by comfort?)

2. What memories, wounds, or desires from my past still influence my choices today?

   (Are there places I've mistaken nostalgia for God's voice?)

3. Am I ignoring any warnings that the Holy Ghost or trusted counsel has already given me?

   (What signs of danger have I been too sentimental to confront?)

4. What does healthy, godly love actually look like—and do I have that?

   (Does this relationship push me closer to Christ or pull me further from consecration?)

5. Do I feel more spiritually alive or spiritually weakened in this relationship?

   (Is this connection sharpening my discernment or draining my devotion?)

Reflective Summary:

Love can be holy or hypnotic. God's love purifies; counterfeit love pacifies. The difference is discernment.

When love becomes a lie, it doesn't always come through rebellion—it often comes through reconnection. The enemy studies the places where you once felt safest and re-introduces an imitation wrapped in familiarity.

This chapter reminds us that not every reconciliation is restoration. Some are recycled temptations wearing yesterday's perfume.

The man of God must learn to test affection by assignment and chemistry by covenant.

True love strengthens your calling; false love silences it. True covenant multiplies fruit; false covenant multiplies frustration.

When you are tied but not joined, peace disappears, purpose drifts, and discernment dims. But the grace of God still unties what emotion entangled.

If you have ever mistaken relief for restoration, hope remains. God still heals, restores, and realigns.

Let this be your moment of freedom.

Wisdom Key: *God never meant for love to cost you your clarity.*

Prayer:

Lord, open my eyes.

Deliver me from every counterfeit connection and every emotional tie that dulls my discernment.

Expose what pretends to love me but secretly limits me.

Give me strength to walk away from what You never joined and courage to wait for what You have ordained.

Restore my purity of purpose, renew my mind, and re-ignite my devotion.

Teach me to love in truth, to choose in wisdom, and to live in obedience.

In Jesus' mighty name, Amen.

Chapter 8: The School of Recovery- When the Battle Becomes the Lesson

"But I have prayed for thee, that thy faith fail not: and when thou art converted, strengthen thy brethren."

— Luke 22: 32

From Destruction to Discipleship

Every battle is a classroom.

Every wound has a workbook.

And every failure, if surrendered to God, becomes a lecture in discernment.

I have come to realize that every attack of the enemy was never meant merely to destroy the innocent—it was permitted to develop them.

God allows some storms not to sink us, but to school us.

He lets the trap tighten so that discernment can mature.

What once humiliated you will one day educate you.

That's why survivors of spiritual warfare are not victims—they are graduates.

The Curriculum of Pain

The School of Recovery is not held in sanctuaries; it's held in secret places—after betrayal, after heartbreak, after the voice of Delilah has faded and the silence of God feels deafening.

Its syllabus includes:

- **Humility 101** — Learning to Listen Again

- **Discernment 202** — Recognizing Familiar Spirits in New Faces

- **Restoration 303** — Serving Without Bitterness

- **Faith 404** — Believing While Bleeding

The tuition is high, but the diploma is eternal wisdom.

Wisdom Key: *Pain becomes prophecy when you let God interpret it.*

Samson's Second Semester

Samson's greatest miracle didn't happen while he was strong—it happened while he was blind.

Only after losing his sight did, he gain his vision.

In that dark prison, he enrolled in the School of Recovery.

He learned that God's mercy can grow hair again. That calling is not cancelled by compromise when repentance is real.

That the same hands that once held a jawbone can still pull-down strongholds.

What looked like humiliation was heaven's higher education.

Peter and the Class of Grace

Peter failed publicly but graduated privately.

He denied Christ three times—then met grace three times at the shoreline:

"Do you love Me?" "Feed My sheep."

God didn't expel Peter from ministry; He re-enrolled him in mercy. The rooster wasn't judgment—it was the school bell announcing a new beginning.

Wisdom Key: *Grace is God repeating the lesson until obedience passes the test.*

My Own Enrollment

Looking back, I see that every heartbreak, every betrayal, every false love, and every sleepless night was an enrollment form signed by the hand of God.

The devil meant it for destruction, but the Lord turned it into instruction.

I learned that discernment is sharpened by disappointment. That love without wisdom is expensive.

That anointing without accountability is dangerous. And that sometimes God will let you be broken so that others can be built.

The Five Stages of Spiritual Recovery

1. **Recognition** — Admitting that what felt like love was really a lesson.

2. **Repentance** — Turning from deception and returning to discipline.

3. **Release** — Letting go of emotional residue that keeps the wound open.

4. **Rebuilding** — Restoring the altar, the focus, and the boundaries.

5. **Redeployment** — Using the testimony to strengthen others.

The classroom of pain produces graduates who can mentor the next generation.

Application: How to Stay Graduated

- Stay teachable even after you recover; pride will re-enroll you in old lessons.

- Keep journals of revelation; every scar is a syllabus.

- Surround yourself with peers who correct, not cheer your compromise.

- Thank God for what you survived instead of resenting what you lost.

Wisdom Key: *The proof that you've learned is that you no longer repeat the same course.*

Transition to Chapter 9

Every lesson in the School of Recovery prepares you for re-assignment. God never wastes pain; He promotes through it. The same battle that humbled you has now qualified you. You are not the same man who entered the storm—you are wiser, slower to trust, quicker to pray, and anchored in obedience.

When the devil aimed to destroy your ministry, God was secretly developing your maturity. The fire that once burned you now forges you. The tears that once blurred your vision now baptize your purpose.

The next chapter reveals what happens after recovery—when God restores strength, renews discernment, and releases you back into destiny. This is where the graduate of suffering becomes the teacher of grace.

Reflective Questions:

1. What repeated battles might actually be lessons I've resisted learning?

2. Where have I mistaken punishment for training?

3. Which painful experiences revealed the most about God's faithfulness?

4. How can I use what I've learned to strengthen others walking through deception or heartbreak?

5. What new disciplines must I adopt to ensure I don't re-enroll in yesterday's tests?

Reflective Summary:

The School of Recovery teaches that failure is not final—it is **developmental.**

Satan intended to destroy you, but God intended to develop you.

- Every betrayal exposed your need for boundaries.

- Every heartbreak purified your motives.

- Every disappointment trained your discernment.

The classroom of suffering graduates' prophets who walk softly, preach wisely, and love purely.

You are not defined by where you fell but by what you learned when you got up.

Wisdom Key: *The scars of yesterday are the credentials of tomorrow.*

Prayer:

Father, thank You for turning my warfare into wisdom.

Thank You for allowing what hurt me to teach me.

I surrender every painful memory to Your classroom of grace.

Use my story to strengthen others who are still in recovery.

Help me to see instruction where I once saw injustice, and purpose where I once saw pain.

Graduate me from bitterness into blessing, from regret into revelation, from falling into faith.

In Jesus' name, Amen.

Chapter 9: Rebuilt for the Call

"But the God of all grace, who hath called us unto his eternal glory by Christ Jesus, after that ye have suffered a while, make you perfect, stablish, strengthen, settle you."

— 1 Peter 5:10

There comes a point after every storm when God doesn't just comfort you — He begins to rebuild you.

But just as the breaking down of you wasn't glamorous so the rebuilding of you isn't glamorous either. It's not fast. It's not clean. *It's the slow, deliberate process of letting God put your life back together piece by piece after everything that defined you has fallen apart.*

Rebuilding means facing what you ignored, forgiving what hurt you, and surrendering what you can't fix. It's not for the faint of heart; it's for the yielded—those willing to let God reconstruct what pride, pain, and people have torn down.

And through it all, you must choose **to think positively.** Not with empty optimism, but with faith-based focus: believing that if God allowed the breaking, He also intends the building.

Positive thinking in the Holy Ghost doesn't deny the difficulty—it declares that the story isn't over yet. It's the voice that says, *"Something good can still come out of this."*

After betrayal. After divorce. After the silence of family and friends who didn't believe you. After the ministry you poured into walked away.

That's where the true rebuilding begins — not when the pain is over, but when you decide that the pain will not have the final word.

This chapter is for the one who has been left to face life alone — the innocent party who still carries the weight of the damage. The one who is learning *to live again, work again, pray again,* and *believe again.*

Recovery is not a garden of roses. It's a battlefield of surrender. Every step forward requires courage, every breath requires faith, and every sunrise requires choosing to live again.

The Shattered Stage

When a marriage ends or a covenant is broken, it doesn't just wound your heart — it shakes your entire identity. You're not just losing a person; you're losing a rhythm, a routine, a sense of belonging.

Everything feels fragile. You go from *"we"* to *"me."* From *"ours"* to *"mine."* From partnership to survival.

It feels unfair, especially when you were faithful — when you *loved sincerely, prayed earnestly, and fought to make it work.* But God never wastes pain. Even in ruin, there is revelation.

Wisdom Key: *What breaks you in one season becomes what builds you in the next.*

The breaking exposes the foundation. And once it's revealed, God starts His rebuilding — not with applause, but with alignment.

Faith in Fragments

It's easy to believe God when everything is in order. But when you're standing among the ashes of what used to be, faith becomes less about noise and more about breathing.

There will be nights when you'll whisper, *"Lord, I don't understand."* And Heaven will answer, *"You don't have to understand — just survive."*

Survival is a form of worship. It's saying to hell, **"You didn't win."**

Even in brokenness, God is teaching you how to trust again. Every tear becomes mortar in the wall He's rebuilding. Every prayer you manage to whisper becomes a brick of endurance.

Wisdom Key: *Faith isn't proven by what you build — it's proven by what you rebuild after loss.*

The Need for a Faithful Support System

No one heals alone. God never intended you to recover in isolation. When the dust settles, you need a circle — not of critics, but of carriers.

Find people who will listen and believe you. People who won't use your pain as gossip, but as a reason to intercede.

People who see your anointing through your tears and remind you that the call of God has not changed.

Isolation feeds the enemy. He works in silence and shame. But healing grows in the soil of honest conversation and godly counsel.

Surround yourself with voices that call you forward, not back. Men and women of prayer who carry compassion and discernment.

Wisdom Key: *A safe circle is not made of perfect people — it's made of people who protect purpose.*

The Necessity of Deliverance

Divorce and betrayal do more than wound the heart — they open spiritual doors. The enemy uses trauma as an invitation. Spirits of *rejection, anger, lust, depression,* and *bitterness* will attach themselves to pain if they are not confronted.

That's why deliverance is not optional — **it's essential.**

You need men and women of God who will lay hands on you, pray over you, and cast out the spirits that came to stay after the storm.

Deliverance is not about embarrassment; it's about eviction.

It's removing the squatters that pain allowed to live rent-free in your soul.

Don't fear the altar. Don't resist the prayer line. Deliverance is not for the demon-possessed — it's for the demon-harassed.

Wisdom Key: *You can't rebuild with unclean tenants still living in the house.*

Let God cleanse you, not just emotionally, but spiritually. True freedom comes when every chain is named and broken.

The Company You Keep Matters

Healing doesn't just come through who prays for you; it also comes through who walks with you.

When you're recovering, discern your company carefully. Be around people of your same caliber — those who have *depth, accountability,* and *genuine concern for the wounded.*

Avoid those who only want to analyze your past or benefit from your weakness. Seek those who have been through their own valleys and know how to help you climb out of yours.

The wrong company will reopen your wounds. The right company will cover them while they heal. **Wisdom Key:** *The spiritually mature don't compete — they complete.*

The Power of Purposeful Occupation

When your heart is shattered, your mind wants to stop. But movement is part of healing.

Work again. Learn again. Build again. Go back to school. Volunteer. Start over. Not to prove yourself — but to rebuild rhythm.

Work restores focus. Learning rekindles hope. Purpose resets the mind.

Wisdom Key: *An idle mind is the devil's invitation; a purposeful life is God's protection.*

Even small steps — a class, a job, a project — can restore dignity and direction. As you work, pray for discernment in your connections. Not everyone who offers help is sent by Heaven. Some are sent to distract.

But don't let fear of betrayal make you motionless. Healing happens through movement. Every act of discipline declares, *"I'm still here."*

The Stewardship of the Body

When rebuilding begins, God doesn't just restore your soul — He also teaches you to care for your body.

Your health matters. Your diet matters. Your rest matters. A sick body cannot sustain a strong spirit.

After the storm, survival begins with stewardship. **Eat right.** Choose foods that energize rather than drain. Avoid the habits that numb your pain but starve your purpose.

See the doctor. Get your checkups. Take your medication if prescribed. These are not signs of weak faith — they are acts of obedience and wisdom.

Exercise regularly. Walk, stretch, or move your body daily. Physical strength renews mental strength. Elijah was fed and allowed to rest before God sent him back into ministry **(1 Kings 19)**. Likewise, your body needs fuel and recovery to fulfill divine purpose.

Wisdom Key: *Ignoring your health is not humility — it's poor stewardship of grace.*

Care for the temple God has given you. You can't cast out devils if you can't climb a flight of stairs. You can't preach freedom if you're too weary to stand.

Take care of yourself. Survival is not selfish — it's preparation for assignment.

The Call Reconfirmed

When you've walked through loss, deliverance, and rebuilding, something remarkable happens: God starts speaking again.

You begin to hear His voice differently — *clearer, deeper, steadier*. The noise of pain begins to fade, and purpose begins to return.

You realize that what the devil meant for destruction, God meant for instruction. Every wound became a classroom. Every heartbreak, a teacher.

Wisdom Key: *You were not rebuilt to remain silent; you were rebuilt to speak with authority.*

The call didn't die in the fire — it was refined in it.

And now, standing on the other side of pain, you're not who you were. You're wiser, stronger, and more discerning. The storm didn't end you — it educated you.

Reflective Questions:

1. Which areas of my life need rebuilding —
   spiritually, emotionally, or physically?

2. Have I truly allowed God to deliver me, or
   am I still carrying hidden pain?

3. Who in my current circle builds me up,
   and who secretly drains me?

4. What practical steps (work, education,
   exercise, self-care) can I take this month
   toward recovery?

5. Am I ready to hear God's voice again —
   not as a victim, but as a vessel rebuilt for
   His call?

Reflective Summary:

Rebuilding after devastation is not easy. It requires honesty, humility, and help. God rebuilds the man He intends to use, but He does it layer by layer: cleansing the heart, casting out the darkness, restoring discipline, and renewing the body.

You can't rebuild in isolation. You need intercessors, deliverers, encouragers, and purpose. You need to move, to rest, to eat right, and to believe again.

What was meant to destroy you became the soil for your growth. You are not defined by who left, but by Who remained.

The God of restoration is not only giving you back your strength — He's preparing you for service again. You are rebuilt for the call.

Prayer:

Father, thank You for never leaving me, even when life fell apart.

Restore my mind, body, and spirit.

Deliver me from every spirit that attached itself to my pain.

Send people into my life who care, cover, and counsel with wisdom.

Help me stay disciplined — in my eating, my working, my resting, and my praying. Let me never confuse survival with stagnation; keep me moving, building, and believing.

Lord, make me whole again — not who I was before the storm, but who You called me to be after it.

In Jesus' name, Amen.

Chapter 10: From Wounded to Weapon — Walking in Wisdom After the War

"Blessed be the Lord my strength, which teacheth my hands to war, and my fingers to fight."

— Psalm 144:1

The Call After the Storm

You don't come out of a storm the same way you went in.

If you allow the Holy Ghost to finish His work, the very thing that wounded you becomes the weapon God uses to heal others.

Every tear becomes training. Every betrayal becomes strategy. Every failure becomes fire.

God never wastes pain—He recycles it for purpose.

You've been through warfare few could understand, but you survived for a reason.

You are not a casualty; you are a soldier under reconstruction.

What the enemy thought would silence you has only sharpened your discernment.

Wisdom Key: *Before God can trust you with public power, He must first test you with private pain.*

The Graduation of Pain

There's a difference between being hurt and being healed enough to help.

You know you've graduated from pain when the memory no longer paralyzes you—it instructs you.

When you can talk about what broke you without bitterness, and pray for the one who betrayed you without needing an apology.

The moment your pain starts teaching you instead of tormenting you, your weapon is being forged.

Wisdom Key: *Every scar God leaves visible is a sermon someone else needs to hear.*

You survived so someone else could know it's possible. Your story has become your sword.

Trained by Tribulation

True warriors aren't born on the battlefield—they're built in the breaks between.

God trained David in caves before He crowned him.

He trained Joseph in prison before He placed him in the palace.

He trained Paul in the desert before He sent him
to the nations.

And He trained you through *heartbreak,
loneliness,* and *misunderstood silence.*

The nights you cried yourself to sleep became
your classroom.

The mornings you forced yourself to get up
became your drills.

The days you had no one but God became your
boot camp.

You didn't fail the test—you finished it.

Now the Lord is promoting you to another level of spiritual authority.

The Anointing After the Affliction

Oil is not released until something is crushed.

Your anointing increased not because you shouted louder, but because you survived deeper.

You know what it means to worship *while bleeding, to serve while misunderstood, to preach while broken.*

That's why demons now recognize your voice differently.

Your authority was purchased through agony.

Hell knows your name—not because you fell, but because you got back up.

Wisdom Key: *The same hands that once trembled in pain now tremble under power.*

Walking in Wisdom After the War

Getting strong again isn't the goal—staying wise is.

Strength without wisdom is dangerous.

Restoration without repentance is short-lived.

Deliverance without discipline is just a delay before destruction.

Some men don't need another miracle—they need memory.

They need to remember the pain, the distance from God, the humiliation that sin brought, and the tears they cried in secret.

Forgetting the fall is what makes you repeat it.

You don't go back to Delilah once you've been delivered.

You don't entertain Jezebel just because she changed her tone.

When God brings you out, don't you dare go back in.

Wisdom Key: *Strength without strategy is self-destruction in disguise.*

The Watchman Mentality

After God restores you, He expects you to become a watchman over your own life.

That means you stay alert and guard your gates— *your eyes, your ears, your heart,* and *your emotions.*

Ask yourself hard questions:

- Why am I drawn to this again?

- What open door needs to be shut?

- What boundary needs to be reinforced?

A wise man doesn't keep playing with fire once he's been burned.

He doesn't flirt with temptation, thinking grace will cover what discipline should prevent.

Grace forgives—but grace also empowers you to flee.

Wisdom Key: God didn't restore you so you could repeat the lesson—He restored you so you could teach it.

Forged in Fire

Before a sword is sharp, it's first placed in the fire.

Heat reveals impurities. Pressure shapes the blade. Hammering gives it form.

That's what God has done in you.

The fire wasn't punishment—it was formation.

The hammering wasn't rejection—it was refinement.

Now the blade is balanced—tempered, tested, trustworthy.

The same hands that once trembled from loss now hold a weapon of intercession and discernment.

Wisdom Key: *Refinement becomes readiness when you stop fighting the fire.*

The Purpose of the Pain

The pain you survived wasn't random—it was redemptive.

God was sculpting your soul for service.

He allowed betrayal to expose what pride hid.

He let heartbreak teach you discernment.

Every failure revealed a flaw; every flaw became a focus; every focus led you to freedom.

You don't just have strength—you have strategy.

You don't just have a story—you have stewardship.

The New Mantle

When Samson's hair began to grow again, his strength returned—but his vision was new.

He no longer fought for pride; he fought for purpose.

That's where you are now.

The old you died in Delilah's lap, but the new you is rising in God's hands.

This mantle isn't about fame—it's about function.

It's about redeeming time and rescuing others still trapped where you used to be.

Wisdom Key: *Don't just get strong—get wise. Don't just recover—become rooted. Don't just be anointed—be accountable.*

You are not the same man. *You're wiser, humbler, stronger, and more spiritually alert.*

You've been rebuilt for the call—and now you're being released for the mission.

Final Warning

The devil isn't intimidated by your shout—he's threatened by your obedience.

He knows that a man who's been through hell and come out holy is a man who will shake nations.

Don't just shout about your comeback—live it.

Walk circumspectly. Guard your gates. Protect your anointing.

Because the next time the enemy shows up, he should find a man who's not just back on his feet, but a man who knows how to stand.

You are from wounded to weapon—and now you walk in wisdom after the war.

Reflective Questions:

1. What patterns or people must I now separate from in order to stay free?

2. Have I learned from my last fall—or am I walking in circles?

3. How can my scars remind me of grace without making me careless?

4. What boundaries guard my eyes, heart, and mind?

5. Do I walk in wisdom, or just rely on grace to cover what discipline should prevent?

Reflective Summary:

This chapter confronts the danger of spiritual amnesia. Many men fall again because they forget what their last fall cost them.

Restoration without reflection breeds' repetition. Getting back up isn't the end—walking wisely is.

God doesn't just want your strength; He wants your stewardship. The truly wise man remembers *the pain, respects the process,* and *rebuilds with discernment.*

You have been wounded, forged, refined, and re-anointed. Now your mission is to live what you've learned and guard what you've gained.

You are strong again—but you also walk in wisdom after the war.

Prayer:

Lord, thank You for restoring me when I didn't deserve it. Thank You for pulling me out of the pit I once fell into.

Now give me the wisdom to never return. Strengthen my discipline where I was once weak.

Let my scars remind me of grace—and let Your grace empower my obedience. Teach me to walk circumspectly, to guard my anointing, and to live like a man who's been through fire and come out wiser.

I declare that I am strong again, walking in wisdom, and fully armed as the weapon You have forged for this generation.

In Jesus' name, Amen.

Chapter 11: The Rebuilt Man — Standing Guard at the Gates

"Keep thy heart with all diligence; for out of it are the issues of life."

— Proverbs 4:23

There comes a point in every man's healing when God says, *"Now stand guard."*

You've been wounded, *yes.* You've been rebuilt, *yes.* But now comes the watchman's call — to protect what you've been restored to.

Deliverance brought you out of bondage, but discipline keeps you out.

Restoration gave you back your footing, but wisdom keeps you standing.

And vigilance ensures you'll never again lose what God had to resurrect through fire and tears.

You are no longer the broken man begging for mercy — you are the rebuilt man entrusted with *responsibility*. Heaven has healed you; now you must guard the gates.

1. The Gates of a Man

Every man has gates — spiritual entry points that either protect or expose his destiny.

Your *eyes, ears, mouth,* and *heart* are not casual features — they are spiritual borders.

The **eyes** are gates of vision.

The **ears** are gates of influence.

The **mouth** is a gate of authority.

The **heart** is the central gate — the throne room where decisions are made.

Satan doesn't need to destroy the house if he can get through the gate.

That's why Scripture warns: *"He that hath no rule over his own spirit is like a city that is broken down, and without walls."*

(Proverbs 25:28)

If you leave your gates unguarded, your **anointing** will leak, your **discernment** will dull, and your **purpose** will be plundered again.

2. Guarding the Eye Gate

The eye is the window to the soul — but it's also the door through which deception enters.

The strange woman didn't need to cast a spell; she just needed to be seen.

That's why Job said, *"I made a covenant with mine eyes."* **(Job 31:1)**

The rebuilt man watches what he watches. He understands that what entertains him will eventually shape him.

He no longer flirts with images that provoke old appetites. He trains his eyes to look beyond appearance and discern spirit.

Wisdom Key: *A pure gaze keeps the heart clean. What you behold, you will eventually believe.*

3. Guarding the Ear Gate

Faith comes by hearing — but so does failure.

Who you listen to will determine what you live by.

The strange woman flatters with her lips.

She whispers affirmation that feels good but carries poison.

The rebuilt man must discern the difference between comfort and counsel.

Not every voice deserves your attention — especially after deliverance.

Some voices sound compassionate but carry compromise.

Wisdom Key: *The ear that entertains deception soon obeys destruction.*

Surround yourself with men and women who sharpen, not seduce; who challenge, not charm.

If their words weaken your conviction, they are an open gate to confusion.

4. Guarding the Mouth Gate

Death and life are in the power of the tongue

(Proverbs 18:21).

You can't rebuild your future if you keep rehearsing your failures.

The rebuilt man speaks **life** — not lust, not bitterness, not regret. He no longer defends his past; he declares his purpose.

Every time you speak, you either build a wall of protection or open a door to attack. Your words are weapons. Use them wisely.

Wisdom Key: *The rebuilt man's speech becomes his safeguard. What he declares daily, he eventually becomes.*

5. Guarding the Heart Gate

The heart is the command center of destiny.

That's why Solomon said, *"Keep thy heart with all diligence."*

Because out of it flow the issues of life — your direction, your discernment, and your devotion.

The heart, once broken, must be retrained. You cannot rebuild your life if you still feed your wounds.

The rebuilt man **forgives** quickly, **loves** cautiously, and **trusts** only under God's instruction.

He knows that emotional hunger is the most dangerous appetite of all.

Guarding the heart means letting the Holy Ghost filter every attachment, every affection, and every ambition.

Wisdom Key: *A guarded heart does not mean a hardened heart. It means a healed one that refuses to reopen old wounds.*

6. The Watchman's Role

Every rebuilt man becomes a watchman — not just for himself, but for others. You've been trained by tears. You've earned your discernment in the dark.

Now God calls you to stand on the wall — *to warn, to pray, to intercede.* The same pain that once humbled you now gives you authority to help others.

When you see another man drifting toward Delilah's lap, you speak up. When you discern the pattern in someone's life that almost destroyed yours, you sound the alarm.

You are not paranoid — you are prepared.

Wisdom Key: *The watchman's burden is not fear; it's foresight. He sees danger before others do.*

7. The Guard's Routine

To remain rebuilt, you must stay disciplined.

- **Pray daily** — don't wait for temptation to remind you to talk to God.

- **Study the Word** — Scripture is not optional reading; it's your manual for survival.

- **Stay accountable** — isolation invites infiltration.

- **Serve others** — humility keeps pride from rebuilding your old prison.

- **Maintain your boundaries** — what cost you last time will kill you next time if you're careless.

The man who stands guard doesn't live in fear; he lives in focus.

8. The Season of Singleness

If you can avoid it, don't date or see anyone until you are fully healed and grounded in the Word of God.

Healing takes time. Deliverance takes discipline. And discernment takes development.

Too many men rush into new relationships trying to prove they've "moved on," when in truth, they're still bleeding under the surface.

A relationship started in recovery often becomes another form of relapse. Until you can stand strong without validation, you're not ready to love from a place of strength.

You don't heal by replacing people — you heal by returning to God.

Let the Holy Ghost rebuild your confidence, not someone's compliments.

Let the Word of God become your counselor, not a new connection.

Let prayer become your intimacy before you seek partnership.

The season of singleness is not punishment — it's preparation.

It's where God rebuilds your discernment, rewires your desires, and restores your peace.

Wisdom Key: *Healing before dating is not isolation — it's insulation. God hides you to help you, not to hurt you.*

Transition into Chapter 12

Once the man is rebuilt and standing guard, God begins to reassign him.

Healing is never the final stage—it is the launching pad for divine purpose. The same man who once stumbled now becomes a soldier under command. The same voice that once cried in brokenness now speaks with authority. The same hands that once reached for comfort now carry power to comfort others.

When God restores a man, He does not merely return him to what he was; He advances him to what he was always meant to be. Rebuilding is not just about survival—it is about stewardship. You have been healed to help. You have been delivered to deliver.

And now, the Lord says: *"It's time to stand not only at the gates of your own life, but at the gates of destiny for others."*

Reflective Questions:

1. Which of my gates — eyes, ears, mouth, or heart — is most vulnerable right now?

2. Who in my circle strengthens my discernment, and who weakens it?

3. What daily habits can I build to keep my gates guarded?

4. Have I truly forgiven the past, or am I still living in reaction to it?

5. How can I help guard another man who's walking the same road I once did?

Reflective Summary:

The rebuilt man is not defined by his past; he's disciplined by it.

He stands guard over the gates of his soul, knowing that the battle is no longer external — it's internal.

The same gates that once invited destruction now protect destiny.

You are not just healed — you are assigned.

Your scars have become your sentinels, your discipline your defense, and your discernment your armor.

Every gate you guard is another generation you protect.

Prayer:

Father,

Thank You for rebuilding me after the ruins.

Teach me to guard what You've restored.

Help me to stay alert — not in fear, but in faith.

Let my eyes stay pure, my ears tuned to truth, my words seasoned with grace, and my heart anchored in holiness.

Make me a watchman over my life and over others You've called me to protect.

Let no strange spirit, flattering tongue, or deceptive desire breach these gates again.

I am rebuilt, restored, and ready — by Your Spirit and for Your glory.

In Jesus' name, Amen.

Chapter 12: Reassigned by God — Walking in Purpose After Deliverance

"And after you have suffered a little while, the God of all grace, who has called you to His eternal glory in Christ, will Himself restore, confirm, strengthen, and establish you."

— 1 Peter 5:10

When a man has been rebuilt, heaven does not leave him standing still.

God begins to reassign him. Healing was the training ground; obedience is the next campaign.

The same man who once fought for survival now fights for souls. The same mouth that once confessed defeat now decrees deliverance.

The same tears that once represented pain now water the ground of someone else's promise.

The rebuilt man becomes a sent man.

He carries evidence of grace—scars that speak, discipline that guards, and discernment that leads. The wilderness was never wasted; it was a workshop. Every tear was a lesson. Every temptation was a test. Every fall was a classroom where God taught you to walk again.

Now, you walk not as a casualty, but as a commander—one who has seen the battlefield and lived to tell the story.

1. The Call to Function, Not Fame

Reassignment isn't about being seen—it's about being sent.

God doesn't promote men to platforms; He promotes them to purpose.

The rebuilt man no longer craves recognition; he craves results that glorify Christ. His worth is no longer measured by applause, titles, or relationships, but by obedience.

He understands that his validation comes from the voice that called him out of darkness, not from the crowd that once misunderstood him.

This is what the world can't comprehend: the man who has been through fire doesn't live to be famous—he lives to be faithful.

Wisdom Key: *God never restores you to where you were—He repositions you for where He needs you.*

2. Serving from the Scar

Your scars are not disqualifications; they are qualifications. You are most effective where you were once afflicted.

The pain that nearly destroyed you becomes the map that guides others home. When you speak, you carry the sound of someone who has been there—and that makes your words prophetic and piercing.

When you testify, hell listens, because your scars remind the enemy that he failed.

When you pray, heaven responds, because your tears carry history.

When you worship, it's not performance—it's remembrance.

Your scars have become sermons, your discipline has become your defense, and your deliverance has become your ministry.

Wisdom Key: Only healed men can lead hurting men out of bondage.

3. A Soldier's March Forward

Reassignment comes with *responsibility.* The moment God says, *"Go,"* you must move with *focus* and *humility.*

Stay alert to the orders of the Spirit. Don't rebuild what God has burned down. Don't chase what He has closed. Don't return to places where your discernment once died.

Forward motion requires letting go of backward attachments.

That means releasing the old version of yourself that still tries to prove something.

The man you used to be no longer exists. Stop mourning him.

You were not healed to relive your history; you were healed to rewrite it.

Wisdom Key: *The same obedience that delivered you must now direct you.*

4. Mentorship: The Legacy of the Rebuilt Man

Reassignment isn't only vertical—it's horizontal.

What God did in you; He now wants to do through you.

The rebuilt man becomes a mentor—a spiritual father, a counselor, a builder of men.

He reaches for those who are walking the same dark road he once did and says, *"Follow me as I follow Christ."*

He becomes what he never had—a voice of truth in a world full of counterfeits.

Your testimony will save lives that sermons can't reach.

The men you help restore will become your spiritual sons—proof that your pain wasn't wasted.

Wisdom Key: *You have survived too much to stay silent. Your healing is someone else's hope.*

5. Guarding Humility in the New Assignment

With every new level of authority comes a new need for humility.

Power without humility is pride in disguise.

The rebuilt man knows that everything he carries—anointing, influence, opportunity—was purchased through mercy.

He doesn't boast; he bows.

He doesn't compare; he consecrates.

The higher you go, the lower you must stay before God.

For pride is the gate that Delilah still knows how to unlock.

The man who forgets that he was once broken will soon be broken again.

Wisdom Key: *Humility is the fence around restored strength.*

6. Staying Faithful in the Ordinary

Reassignment doesn't always look spectacular.

Sometimes it's showing up every day, praying when you don't feel like it, loving when you'd rather withdraw, and staying planted when your flesh wants to wander.

The rebuilt man learns that faithfulness in small things produces fruit in great things.

He stops chasing emotional highs and learns the steady rhythm of obedience.

He builds quietly, prays consistently, and trusts completely.

Wisdom Key: *Maturity is not proven in moments of power—it's proven in seasons of consistency.*

7. The Final Test: Stewardship

God's final test for every rebuilt man is stewardship.

- Can you manage what you once misused?

- Can you handle the blessing that once broke you?

- Can you carry the mantle without turning it into merchandise?

If you can be trusted in secret, God will release you in public.

If you can stay pure in the private spaces, He will increase your platform in the open.

He's not testing your anointing—He's testing your alignment.

Wisdom Key: *The proof of restoration is not power—**it's responsibility.***

Reflective Questions:

1. What new purpose or assignment has God revealed since my restoration began?

2. How am I using my scars to serve others rather than hide them?

3. Am I seeking influence or obedience in my new season?

4. Who can I mentor or disciple from the lessons of my own deliverance?

5. What practical boundaries will keep me humble and grounded as God promotes me?

Reflective Summary:

Reassignment is not about returning—it's about redeeming. God did not rebuild you to sit idle. He restored you to move forward with *focus, discipline,* and *grace.*

You have survived the breaking, endured the rebuilding, and now you walk as a vessel of divine wisdom. The very place that once represented your greatest failure has become your platform for the glory of God.

The rebuilt man is now the reassigned man.

He carries discernment where there was once deception.

He guards the gates where he once gave them away.

And he walks—not as a victim of his past, but as a vessel of God's purpose.

Closing Prayer:

Father,

Thank You for trusting me again. Thank You for the mercy that lifted me, the grace that rebuilt me, and the Spirit that now leads me.

Help me to walk worthy of the assignment You've placed in my hands.

Let my strength serve others. Let my scars speak truth. Keep me humble in victory, steadfast in warfare, and faithful in every season.

Send me where You need me. Use me as Your instrument of healing and holiness.

I am Yours—*reassigned, refined,* and *ready for the work ahead.*

In Jesus' name, Amen.

Afterword: A Warning Born of Purpose

"See then that ye walk circumspectly, not as fools, but as wise."

— Ephesians 5:15

I did not write this book out of pain.

I wrote it out of purpose.

Purpose to warn.

Purpose to awaken.

Purpose to deliver men from the traps I've seen and the spirits I've discerned.

This message is not about bitterness—it's about clarity.

It's a call for men everywhere to stop, think, and consider before they destroy their destiny through disobedience.

Far too many men have traded their calling for comfort, their crown for compromise, and their vision for validation.

They call it love, but it's lust. They call it connection, but it's bondage. They call it grace, but it's deception.

This book was written to sound the alarm—to warn men not to marry the woman the Holy Ghost never sent, not to build with someone who doesn't believe, and not to let their emotions make lifelong decisions that eternity will judge.

The Purpose Behind the Warning

There's a difference between being lonely and being led.

Too many men confuse emotional emptiness with divine leading.

The enemy knows that if he can't defeat a man by force, he will distract him through romance.

It's not that women are the enemy—far from it. God created woman as a helpmate.

But the enemy counterfeits what God consecrates. He disguises destruction as desire.

And when a man ignores the voice of the Holy Ghost for the voice of a seductive spirit, he has already surrendered his authority.

This book is not an attack on women—it's an attack on deception.

It's a call for men to return to spiritual discipline, discernment, and self-control.

To refuse to marry potential and ignore purpose.

To stop seeking companionship before completion.

A Word to the Men

Brothers, I say this with love and urgency: don't ignore the warning signs.

If the woman you're with mocks holiness, dishonors leadership, manipulates your emotions, or pulls you away from your purpose—walk away.

You are not strong enough to fix what the Holy Ghost has already condemned.

You can't deliver her if you're distracted by her.

You can't lead her if you're lusting after her.

You can't guard your anointing if you keep giving your heart to the wrong assignment.

The enemy doesn't need your body—he's after your birthright.

He knows that if he can confuse your heart, he can cancel your destiny.

Don't let him.

The Wake-Up Call

I have seen too many anointed men lose everything—not because they didn't love God, but because they didn't listen to God.

They ignored the warnings. They mistook comfort for confirmation.

They mistook attention for affection.

But when the dust settled, the same woman who once flattered them was the one the enemy used to flatten them.

So, hear me clearly: before you pursue her, pray.

Before you propose, pause.

Before you enter covenant, consult the Counselor—the Holy Ghost.

If God says no, believe Him.

If peace leaves, don't chase it.

If discernment screams, don't silence it.

Because the enemy's trap never looks like a trap—it looks like your type.

A Word to the Church

This message must return to our pulpits.

We cannot keep losing godly men because no one dared to confront the Delilah spirit.

We cannot keep watching homes collapse while the Church stays quiet about sin.

The Church must teach our men how to recognize counterfeit love and confront spiritual manipulation.

We need deliverance ministries that don't just focus on demons—but on discipline.

We need pastors who prepare men for purpose before pushing them toward marriage.

We need accountability restored to leadership, and truth restored to teaching.

The silence of the Church is the success of the serpent.

A Word to the Next Generation

To every young man reading this:

- Don't make the same mistakes my generation made.

- Don't let lust rewrite your legacy.

- Don't waste your youth chasing what will drain your anointing.

Let this book be your warning—and your wisdom.

Don't marry the strange woman. Don't entertain the Jezebel spirit. Don't confuse Delilah's comfort with God's calling.

Be the man who waits. Be the man who watches. Be the man who walks with God.

If you protect your purity, you preserve your power.

If you guard your gates, you guard your greatness.

If you listen to the Holy Ghost, you will not lose your destiny.

A Final Word

I wrote this because I care.

Because I've seen what happens when men ignore the still small voice.

Because I've seen families destroyed, ministries derailed, and callings forfeited—all over the wrong relationship.

But I've also seen the mercy of God.

I've seen Him rebuild, restore, and resurrect the broken.

I've seen men rise from ashes and walk in purpose again.

And I believe that can be your story too—if you choose wisdom.

Don't let lust lead you. Let love from God guide you.

Don't let pressure push you. Let purpose position you.

And don't marry this woman—until you know she was sent by God.

Closing Prayer:

Father,

Thank You for the clarity of truth and the mercy of warning. For every man who will read these words, open his eyes to see beyond attraction and emotion.

Teach him to hear Your voice above his flesh, to wait for confirmation before commitment, and to walk away from anything that compromises his calling.

Raise up a generation of watchful, wise, Spirit-led men. Men who lead with love, live with purity, and walk with power. Men who build homes on holiness and not on hype.

May every deception be exposed, every counterfeit uncovered, and every destiny preserved.

In Jesus' name, Amen.

Note from the Author:

When I first began writing this book, I didn't set out to tell a story of regret or pain — I set out to tell a truth that too many men are too afraid, too ashamed, or too late to tell.

This book was written because I've seen what happens when men of promise marry women without purpose — when anointed men ignore the Holy Ghost for the sake of companionship, and when good intentions collide with ungodly influence.

I've lived long enough to watch ministries collapse, marriages implode, families ruined and men lose their way — not because they were evil, but because they were unaware.

I wrote Brother, Whatever You Do, Please Don't Marry This Woman to confront that blindness.

To warn men before they walk into the trap.

To awaken spiritual leaders who have fallen asleep at the gate.

And to give a voice to those who are silently struggling, ashamed to admit that what they thought was love has become their battlefield.

My hope is that this book will help men rediscover what real strength looks like — not the kind that conquers women, but the kind that conquers weakness.

I want them to know that discipline is not denial, and that delay is not rejection.

Sometimes God says "wait" because He's protecting your purpose, not withholding your pleasure.

I've made mistakes. I've lived through deception, and I've survived the silence that follows destruction. But I'm here to say: you can recover.

You can live again, love again, and lead again — if you choose wisdom first.

To every man reading this:

Don't let lust rewrite your legacy.

Don't let flattery blind your discernment.

And don't marry this woman — until you know she was sent by God.

— Eld Joel Latimore Jr.

About the Author

Eld Joel Latimore Jr. is an author, teacher, and prophetic voice whose ministry centers on faith, holiness, and the transforming power of the Holy Ghost. A man seasoned by both failure and faith, he writes with a shepherd's heart and a soldier's precision—calling men and women back to biblical truth, spiritual discipline, and personal accountability.

Through his books, Elder Latimore exposes the subtle tactics of the enemy that destroy lives, relationships, and ministries from within. His works, including *Faith and Fire: Walking with the Holy Ghost, Black People, the Church, and the Reality of the Holy Ghost, and You Were Born for More: A Journey of Faith, Mentorship, and Purpose,* are written to restore hope, rekindle discernment, and prepare believers for the battles of the last days.

Elder Latimore's writing flows from a life transformed by grace and guided by conviction. His ministry challenges readers to live holy, think soberly, and walk in the Spirit—not in assumption, but in revelation.

When he is not writing or teaching, Elder Latimore mentors' men in *spiritual recovery* and *leadership development*, helping them rediscover their calling, rebuild their confidence, and walk again in the authority of Christ.

He currently resides in the United States, continuing his mission to strengthen the Body of Christ through truth, wisdom, and the power of the Holy Ghost.